TRUE STORIES

Behind the Songs

A HIGH-BEGINNING READER

by Sandra Heyer

PEARSON
Longman

More True Stories Behind the Songs

Pearson Education, 10 Bank Street, White Plains, NY 10606 USA

Staff credits: The people who made up the *More True Stories Behind the Songs* team, representing editorial, production, design, and manufacturing, are Pietro Alongi, John Brezinsky, Dave Dickey, Oliva Fernandez, Christopher Leonowicz, Amy McCormick, Barbara Sabella, Debbie Sistino, and Jennifer Stem.
Development editor: Karen Davy
Photo credits: Cover Shutterstock.com; **Page 2** Shutterstock.com; **4** Ashley Cooper/Corbis; **8** east2west news; **12** Shutterstock.com; **14** Michael S. Yamashita/Corbis; **18** Mark Rucker/Transcendental Graphics/ Getty Images; **21** AP Images/Rich Pedroncelli; **22** iStockphoto.com; **24** David Corio/Getty Images; **28** Paul Joseph Brown/Seattle Post-Intelligencer; **32** Shutterstock.com; **34** Christian Science Monitor/Getty Images; **38** iStockphoto.com; **42** Shutterstock.com; **44** John Van Hasselt/Sygma/Corbis; **47** Shutterstock.com; **48** Teru Kuwayama/Corbis; **52** Shutterstock.com; **54** AP Images/Andrew Milligan; **58** AP Images/Sean Simmers; **62** (top) Shutterstock.com, (bottom) Shutterstock.com; **64** Corbis; **67** National Portrait Gallery, Smithsonian Institution/Art Resource, NY; **68** Shutterstock.com; **72** Gu Yue/ColorChinaPhoto/Newscom; **74** Central Press/ Getty Images; **78** AP Images/Steven Day.
Illustrations: Pages 64 and 68 MacNeill & Macintosh
Song credits: See page 105.
Text composition: Rainbow Graphics
Text font: 12.5 Minion

Library of Congress Cataloging-in-Publication Data

Heyer, Sandra.
  More true stories behind the songs : a high-beginning reader / by Sandra Heyer.
    p. cm.
  ISBN 0-13-246805-0
  1. English language—Textbooks for foreign speakers. 2. Readers. I. Title.
  PE1128.H4359 2011
    428.6'4—dc22

                         2010037522

ISBN-10: 0-13-246805-0
ISBN-13: 978-0-13-246805-3

Printed in the United States of America
4 5 6 7 8 9 10—V011—18 17 16 15

CONTENTS

Introduction v

UNIT 1 FINDING A LOST LOVE 2
    Song: "You're Beautiful" 3
    Story 1: The Angel on the Subway 5
    Story 2: The Return to Borovlyanka 9

UNIT 2 BASEBALL 12
    Song: "Take Me Out to the Ball Game" 13
    Story 3: Baseball Fever 15
    Story 4: Three Strikes—And the Pitcher's Out? ... 19

UNIT 3 SOMEBODY TO LEAN ON 22
    Song: "Lean on Me" 23
    Story 5: A Husband and Father to Lean On 25
    Story 6: A Cup of Coffee and a Kidney to Go 29

UNIT 4 A SIMPLE LIFE 32
    Song: "Simple Gifts" 33
    Story 7: The Last Three? 35
    Story 8: A Wonderful Gift? 39

UNIT 5 THE WAY TO PEACE 42
    Song: "Peace Train" 43
    Story 9: The Professor and the Peace Train 45
    Story 10: Three Cups of Tea 49

UNIT 6 YOU CAN'T JUDGE A BOOK BY ITS COVER 52
    Song: "I Dreamed a Dream" 53
    Story 11: Susan's Got Talent 55
    Story 12: The King in the Nursing Home 59

UNIT 7 GREAT ESCAPES 62
    Song: "Follow the Drinking Gourd" 63
    Story 13: The Drinking Gourd 65
    Story 14: Twelve Kilometers to a New Life 69

UNIT 8 SURVIVORS 72
    Song: "My Heart Will Go On" 73
    Story 15: The Littlest Passenger 75
    Story 16: Miracle on the Hudson 79

To the Teacher 82
Answer Key 100
Acknowledgments 104

INTRODUCTION

More True Stories Behind the Songs is a high-beginning reader for students of English. The book consists of eight units, each focusing on a central theme. The units open with the lyrics to a song, and two true stories follow: The first tells the story behind the song, and the second is related to the theme of the unit. Although the two stories are linked thematically, they can stand on their own; students' success with one does not depend on their having read the other. (And students can complete the units in any order.) The stories are accompanied by carefully-paced pre-and post-reading exercises that develop and build students' language skills.

Teachers have long used songs to enliven their classrooms and develop students' language skills, but as many teachers have discovered, the use of songs in the classroom can be problematic. Songs frequently contain nonstandard grammar as well as abundant low-frequency, archaic, or idiomatic vocabulary. This textbook circumvents those problems by making the song the introduction to the lesson rather than its primary focus. Students need not understand every word or grammatical structure in the song because the stories and exercises that follow are the fundamental vehicles for language learning.

More True Stories Behind the Songs can be used in tandem with *More True Stories.* It is written at the same level but has all new stories and exercises, as well as the addition of songs. Why does the *True Stories* series offer two high-beginning readers? First, some students need more time at this level before moving on to *Even More True Stories,* the next book in the series. *More True Stories Behind the Songs* gives students the option of lingering awhile at this level. They can go back and forth between *More True Stories Behind the Songs* and *More True Stories,* or they can complete one book and then the other. (Students can read either book first.) Second, a choice of two books helps veteran teachers keep their lessons fresh: They can use *More True Stories* one semester and *More True Stories Behind the Songs* the next. Alternating between the two books also keeps the lessons fresh for students who choose to stay in a high-beginning class when their classmates move on to the next level. They can essentially repeat the class but with all new material.

Following are some suggestions for using *More True Stories Behind the Songs.* Teachers new to the field might find these suggestions especially helpful. Please remember that these are only suggestions. Teachers should, of course, feel free to adapt these strategies to best suit their teaching styles and their students' learning styles. In a special "To the Teacher" section at the back of the book, there are many more easy-to-use suggestions for activities, as well as additional background information on each story and song.

THE SONG

In this section, you will find the lyrics to the song. The lyrics correspond to the recordings by performers recommended under "About the Song" in the To the Teacher section, so it is best to play that recording of the song for the class. (If you choose performances by different recording artists, please be aware that the lyrics might differ slightly.) You can find the songs on commercially produced CDs (many of which are available at public libraries) or on your favorite website as downloadable recordings. At *www.pearsonlongman.com/truestories*, you will find a link that connects you to the recommended recordings in iTunes.

Both preceding and following the lyrics are exercises that enhance students' understanding and enjoyment of the song. The songs open the door to innumerable opportunities for expansion. Students can share related songs from their native countries; they can listen to more songs by the same songwriter, by the same singer, from the same era, or on the same topic; and they can watch performances of the song on the Internet. The songs in this book were chosen because of their compelling back-stories, staying power, and musical or historical significance. If you teach teenagers or young adults, you may wish to follow up and expand on the units' themes by listening to additional songs that appeal especially to that age group.

PRE-READING

This section consists of questions that guide students as they describe the photo and share experiences related to the topic.

If your students need extra support, consider telling them the gist of the story before they read it. As you tell the story, illustrate it on the board. Only a few simple sketches can have a dramatic effect on subsequent reading comprehension, so this pre-reading activity is well worth the five or ten minutes you devote to it. If you're not skilled at drawing—and many of us are not—please see the drawing tips in the To the Teacher section. Also in the To the Teacher section are many suggestions for pre-, during-, and post-reading activities.

READING

Immediately preceding the first story is a simple explanation of how the song and story are connected. They are related in one of two ways:

- The song is autobiographical, and the story recounts the experience that prompted the songwriter to write it.
- The story explains the connection between the song and a historical era or cultural phenomenon.

Preceding the second story is a short explanation of how the second story is related to the first.

Go to *www.pearsonlongman.com/truestories* for audio recordings (mp3 files) of all of the stories.

THE EXERCISES

Following each story are three types of exercises: vocabulary, comprehension, and discussion/writing. Students can complete the exercises individually, in pairs, in small groups, or with the whole class. The exercises can be completed in class or assigned as homework. At the back of the book, there is an answer key to the exercises.

VOCABULARY

The vocabulary exercises highlight words that ESL students identified as new and that could be clearly drawn, described, or defined. The exercises clarify meaning while giving students practice in establishing meaning through contextual clues. In the To the Teacher section, there are suggestions for supplemental vocabulary activities.

COMPREHENSION

The comprehension exercises test students' understanding of the story; more important, the exercises help students develop reading skills they will use throughout their reading careers—skills such as scanning, summarizing, identifying the main idea, and recognizing connectors and other rhetorical devices.

DISCUSSION/WRITING

The discussion/writing exercises require students to complete a task—to fill in a chart, to interview a classmate, to draw a picture or a map—so that there is a concrete focus to the activity. The task-centered exercises make it possible for students to talk without the direct supervision of the teacher, a necessity in large classes. The exercises always require students to write before speaking. Even if students are inexperienced writers, it is important not to skip this step. Generally, students talk more if they have had a chance to collect their thoughts in writing first, even if they are able to write only words and phrases. Students who are fairly accomplished writers may need more challenging assignments, such as writing short paragraphs. Students who are less experienced writers may need to see some sample responses before they write.

The vocabulary, comprehension, discussion, and writing exercises are at approximately parallel levels; that is, they assume that students speak and write about as well as they read. Of course, that is not always the case. Please feel free to modify the exercises—to adjust them up or down to suit students' proficiency levels, to skip some, or to add some of your own.

Both the exercises and reading selections are intended to build students' confidence along with their reading skills. Above all, it is hoped that reading *More True Stories Behind the Songs* will be a pleasure, for both you and your students.

FINDING A
LOST LOVE

THE SONG

- Close your book and listen to the song. As you listen, write some of the words and phrases you understand on your own paper. Then share your words with the class. What do you think the song is about?

- The title of the song is "You're Beautiful." Who is the beautiful person in the song? Take a guess.

- The songwriter says he saw an angel. The word *angel* has two meanings. One meaning is religious, and the other meaning is not religious. Discuss the two meanings of the word *angel*.

- Now open your book and listen to the song again. Read the words as you listen.

YOU'RE BEAUTIFUL

My life is brilliant.

My life is brilliant.
My love is pure.
I saw an angel,
Of that I'm sure.
She smiled at me on the subway.
She was with another man,
But I won't lose no sleep on that
'Cause[1] I've got a plan.

You're beautiful. You're beautiful.
You're beautiful, it's true.
I saw your face in a crowded place,
And I don't know what to do
'Cause I'll never be with you.

Yeah, she caught my eye
As we walked on by.
She could see from my face that I was
Flying high.
And I don't think that I'll see her again,
But we shared a moment that will last
  'til[2] the end.

You're beautiful. You're beautiful.
You're beautiful, it's true.
I saw your face in a crowded place,
And I don't know what to do
'Cause I'll never be with you.

You're beautiful. You're beautiful.
You're beautiful, it's true.
There must be an angel with a smile on
  her face
When she thought up that I should be
  with you.
But it's time to face the truth—
I will never be with you.

- **Listen to the song again. Lip-sync[3] the words as you listen.**

---

[1] **'Cause:** because

[2] **'til:** until

[3] **Lip-sync:** to pretend you are singing—to move your lips, but not speak; pronounced "lip-sink"

1 PRE-READING

Look at the picture.

➤ What city is this? (What are some possible cities?)

➤ Do you ride the subway sometimes? Have you had an interesting experience on the subway? If so, tell the class about it.

2 READING

James Blunt wrote the song "You're Beautiful." Who was the woman James saw on the subway? Was she a stranger, someone James knew, or someone James imagined?

Read the story to find out.

THE ANGEL ON THE SUBWAY

When James Blunt was a university student, he had a girlfriend named Sarah. She was smart and funny, and James loved her. "Maybe someday I'll marry Sarah," he often thought.

After James graduated from the university, he joined the British Army. At first, he kept in touch with Sarah; he called her and e-mailed her whenever he could. But then the army sent him to other countries—to Kosovo and then to Switzerland—and it was difficult to call and send e-mail. Months went by, then years went by, and James lost touch with Sarah. He had no idea where she was.

While he was in the army, James played his guitar in his free time. Sometimes he wrote songs and sang them while he played his guitar. Whenever he sang, other soldiers came and listened to him. "You have talent," his friends in the army told him. "You should be a musician."

When James got out of the army, he decided to work as a songwriter and professional musician. It wasn't easy. He wrote a lot of songs and played his guitar in a lot of small clubs in London, but he didn't make a lot of money. He needed a big hit to make him famous.

One day James got on a subway train in London, and there she was: Sarah. She was standing only a few feet away from James. James smiled at her, and she smiled back. Then James noticed that Sarah was with another man. Was the man Sarah's boyfriend? Was he her fiancé? Was he her husband? James didn't know, but he did know this: Sarah was in love with someone else.

James and Sarah looked at each other for a second or two. Neither moved, and neither spoke. Then the train came into the next station. Sarah and the man got off the train and disappeared into the crowd.

James went straight home and began to write about Sarah. "I saw an angel," he wrote. "Of that I'm sure." He didn't stop writing until his poem about Sarah was finished. Then he picked up his guitar and played music to go with the poem. In only a few hours, he had a complete song.

The song "You're Beautiful" was a number one hit, and it made James famous. And what about Sarah? Did she hear the song on the radio? She probably did, and she probably knew the song was about her. But she never called James, and he never saw her again. Perhaps Sarah is a wife now; perhaps she is a mother. But to James, she will always be the angel on the subway.

3 VOCABULARY

Complete the sentences with the words below.

crowd	fiancé	~~joined~~	keep in touch	lost touch	perhaps

1. James wanted to be a soldier, so he _____ joined _____ the army.

2. James e-mailed Sarah because he wanted to _____.

3. James _____ with Sarah. He had no idea where she was.

4. Maybe Sarah was going to marry the man. Maybe he was her _____.

5. There were a lot of people at the station. Sarah disappeared into the _____.

6. Maybe Sarah is married now; _____ she has children.

4 COMPREHENSION

◆ Understanding the Main Ideas

Circle the letter of the correct answer.

1. The song "You're Beautiful" is about a woman named Sarah, who was
   a. a singer at a club in London.
   b. a stranger James saw on the subway.
   c. James's girlfriend when he was a university student.

2. James didn't speak to Sarah because
   a. she was with another man.
   b. he was with another woman.
   c. she was standing too far away from him.

3. After James saw Sarah on the subway, he
   a. called her and kept in touch.
   b. never saw her again.
   c. asked her to marry him.

◆ Understanding Time Relationships

Find the best way to complete each sentence. Write the letter of your answer on the line.

1. James had a girlfriend named Sarah __b__

2. He called and e-mailed Sarah ____

3. Other soldiers came and listened to him ____

4. Sarah and the man disappeared into the crowd ____

5. James didn't stop writing ____

a. when the train came into the next station.
b. when he was a university student.
c. until his poem was finished.
d. whenever he sang.
e. whenever he could.

◆ **Understanding Details**

One word in each sentence is not correct. Find the word and cross it out.
Write the correct word.

1. James joined the British ~~Navy~~ Army.

2. The army sent him to other countries—to Canada and then to Switzerland.

3. James played his violin in his free time.

4. He decided to work as a poet and professional musician.

5. James played his guitar in a lot of big clubs in London.

6. He needed a big hit to make him happy.

7. One day he got on a subway train in Paris and saw Sarah.

8. In only a few days, James wrote a complete song about Sarah.

5 DISCUSSION/WRITING

A. James didn't see Sarah for many years. Then he got on a subway train in London, and there she was. Imagine this: You see a friend that you haven't seen for many years. Your friend says, "Tell me about your life now." What will you tell your friend?

On your own paper, write a paragraph about your life now. For example, you can answer some of these questions in your paragraph. Below the questions is a paragraph one student wrote.

- Where do you live?
- Are you married or single?
- Do you have children? (How many children do you have? Are they boys or girls?)
- What kind of work do you do?
- What do you like to do in your free time?

    I live in Whitewater, Wisconsin, now. I got married ten years ago. I have three children—one boy and two girls. I work in a factory on the assembly line. I like to walk and listen to music—that hasn't changed.

B. Role-play with a partner. Imagine your partner is a friend you haven't seen for years. Tell your partner about your life now.

STORY 2

1 PRE-READING

Look at the pictures.

➤ How old are the man and woman in the small photos?

➤ When do you think the photos were taken?

➤ How do you think the old man and woman in the large photo feel?

➤ Why do they feel that way? (What are some possible reasons?)

➤ Read the title of the story on the next page. Where do you think the village of Borovlyanka is? (What are some possible countries?)

2 READING

In the last story, you read about James and Sarah, a couple who had been apart for several years and then saw each other on the subway. The next story is about another couple. How many years were they apart? Where did they see each other again?

Read the story to find out.

THE RETURN TO BOROVLYANKA

Anna and Boris Kozlov got married on a Saturday afternoon in 1946. The next Tuesday, Boris left home to work in a nearby village. When he returned a few days later, Anna was gone.

Anna and Boris lived in Borovlyanka, a village in Siberia. At that time, Siberia was part of the Soviet Union, and Joseph Stalin was the leader of the country. People who didn't agree with Stalin were executed, imprisoned, or sent to villages that were far from their homes. Anna's father disagreed with Stalin, so Stalin's soldiers took him and his whole family to a faraway village. "Don't go home if you want to live," the soldiers told them.

When neighbors told Boris that soldiers had taken Anna and her family away, he was frantic. For months he went from village to village and looked for her. He couldn't find her.

Meanwhile, Anna's mother was telling her, "Please try to forget Boris. You can never go home, and he will never find you here. You're still young. You can be happy with someone else."

Anna didn't want to forget Boris. He had written her dozens of love letters before they were married, and she still had every one of them. She read them over and over.

One day when Anna was at work, her mother burned Boris's love letters. She burned his photos, too, including their wedding photo. When Anna came home, her mother told her, "A man is coming to see you this evening. I want you to go out with him." Anna shook her head. "No! No!" she cried. "I don't want to go out with another man. I'm married to Boris."

"You will never see Boris again," Anna's mother told her. "Do you want to be alone for the rest of your life?"

Anna went out with the man. Eventually, she married him. Eventually, Boris married someone else, too. But he never forgot Anna, his first love.

The years went by, and Anna and Boris grew old. Anna's husband died, and Boris's wife died. When Anna was 80 years old, she returned to Borovlyanka. She wanted to visit the house where she and Boris had lived together for three days. She was standing near the house when a car stopped across the road. An old man was driving the car. Anna's heart began to pound; the man looked familiar. As he got out of the car, he looked up and saw Anna. He stared at her for a few seconds and then walked toward her. "My darling," he said. "My wife, my life." Anna cried with joy.

The old man was Boris. He had come to Borovlyanka to visit his parents' grave. After 60 years apart, Anna and Boris had returned to Borovlyanka on the same day.

For the next few days, Anna and Boris were inseparable. They talked about the past, and they talked about the future. "Let's get married," Boris said.

A few weeks later, Anna and Boris were husband and wife again.

3 VOCABULARY

Circle the word or words that correctly complete the sentence.

1. A *village* is a small / large town.

2. If you *disagree* with someone, you have the same / a different opinion.

3. If you do something *over and over*, you do it a few / many times.

4. If you *shake your head*, you mean yes / no.

5. Something that happens *eventually* happens after a long / short time.

6. If your heart is *pounding*, it is beating slowly / fast.

7. Someone who is *frantic* is worried / not worried.

8. Someone who cries with *joy* is sad / happy.

4 COMPREHENSION

◆ Understanding Details

Read the summary of the story "The Return to Borovlyanka." There are 12 mistakes in the summary. Find the mistakes and cross them out. Write the correct words. (The first one is done for you.)

Anna and Boris got married in Borovlyanka on a Saturday ~~morning~~ *afternoon* in 1956. The next Friday, Boris left home to work in a faraway village. When he returned a few months later, Anna was gone.

Soldiers had taken Anna and her family away because Anna's brother disagreed with Stalin. For years Boris went from village to village and looked for Anna. He couldn't find her.

Eventually, Anna and Boris married other people. The years went by, and Anna and Boris grew old. Anna's husband died, and Boris's wife died.

When Anna was 60 years old, she returned to Borovlyanka. She wanted to visit the apartment where she and Boris had lived together. On the same day, Boris returned to Borovlyanka to visit his wife's grave.

After 40 years apart, Anna and Boris were together again. A few hours later, they got married.

◆ Understanding Time and Place

Read the phrases from the story. Which phrases tell you *when* something happened? Write them in the *WHEN* column. Which phrases tell you *where* something happened? Write them in the *WHERE* column.

- ~~on a Saturday afternoon~~
- across the road
- in a nearby village
- a few days later

- this evening
- at work
- near the house
- eventually

WHEN	WHERE
on a Saturday afternoon	_____
_____	_____
_____	_____
_____	_____

◆ Understanding Pronouns

Read the words in *italics*. What do they mean? Write the letter of your answer on the line.

1. __c__ *It* was part of the Soviet Union.

2. ____ *He* was the leader of the Soviet Union.

3. ____ *They* were executed, imprisoned, or sent far away.

4. ____ *He* disagreed with Stalin.

5. ____ *They* told Anna's family not to go home.

6. ____ *They* told Boris that soldiers had taken Anna's family away.

7. ____ *She* told Anna to forget Boris.

8. ____ Anna's mother burned *it*.

a. Anna's mother
b. people who disagreed with Stalin
c. Siberia
d. Anna's father
e. neighbors
f. Anna and Boris's wedding photo
g. soldiers
h. Joseph Stalin

5 DISCUSSION/WRITING

A. Anna returned to Borovlyanka. She wanted to visit the house where she and Boris had lived together. Think about a house or an apartment where you lived. What was your favorite room in that home?

On your own paper, draw a picture of your favorite room. You can use circles (○), rectangles (▭), and squares (□) for furniture, but label everything in the room. (For example, you can draw a rectangle for a sofa and write *sofa* on the rectangle.) Then complete the sentences below. Here is what one student wrote.

This was the living room in my home in Paraguay. I liked this room because it was the only room with an air conditioner. The other rooms were hot. Sometimes we all slept in the living room because it was cool.

This was the _____ in my home in _____.
        (name of the room)   (city or country)

I liked this room because _____

_____.

B. Describe your favorite room to a partner. On a separate piece of paper, your partner will draw the room. When you are finished describing the room, show your drawing to your partner. Together, correct any mistakes in your partner's picture.

UNIT 2 BASEBALL

THE SONG

- Tell the class what you know about the game of baseball. Do you know what a *strike* is? Do you know what an *out* is? If you do, tell the class.

- Close your book and listen to the song. The song is about a young woman named Katie Casey. As you listen, write information about Katie on your own paper. (If you can write only a few words about her, that is OK.)

- Now open your book and listen to the song again. Read the words as you listen.

TAKE ME OUT TO THE BALL GAME

Katie Casey was baseball mad.[1]
She had the fever,[2] and she had it bad.
Just to root[3] for the hometown crew,
Every cent—that Katie spent.
On one Saturday, her young beau[4]
Called to see if she'd like to go
To see a show, but Miss Kate said,
"No, I'll tell you what you can do:

Take me out to the ball game.
Take me out with the crowd.
Buy me some peanuts and Cracker
 Jacks.[5]
I don't care if I ever get back
'Cause[6] it's root, root, root for the home
 team.
If they don't win, it's a shame
'Cause it's one, two, three strikes, you're
 out
At the old ball game."

Katie Casey saw all the games.
Knew all the players by their first
 names.
Told the umpire he was wrong
All along, and she was strong.
When the score was two to two,
Katie Casey, she had the clue
To cheer on the boys, she knew just
 what to do.
She made everyone sing this song:

Take me out to the ball game.
Take me out with the crowd.
Buy me some peanuts and Cracker
 Jacks.
I do not care if I ever get back
'Cause it's root, root, root for the home
 team.
If they don't win, it's a shame
'Cause it's one, two, three strikes, you're
 out
At the old ball game.

Take me out to the ball game.
Take me out with the crowd.
Buy me some peanuts and Cracker
 Jacks.
I don't care if I ever get back
'Cause it's root, root, root for the home
 team.
If they don't win, it's a shame
'Cause it's one, two, three strikes, you're
 out
At the old ball game.

- After you read the story on page 15, return to this page and listen to the song again. Sing the verses that begin "Take me out to the ball game." (Don't worry if you can't sing very well; *many* people who sing this song can't sing very well!)

---

[1] **was baseball mad:** loved baseball
[2] **She had the fever:** She was excited.
[3] **root:** cheer
[4] **beau:** boyfriend
[5] **Cracker Jacks:** sweet popcorn mixed with peanuts
[6] **'Cause:** because

1 PRE-READING

Look at the picture.

➤ In which country is this?

➤ What kind of stadium is this?

➤ What are the fans releasing?

➤ Why are they doing that?

2 READING

In almost every baseball stadium in the world, fans stand up during the seventh inning[1] of the game. Then they sing a song together. In the United States, they sing the song "Take Me Out to the Ball Game." Who wrote that song? How did that tradition begin?

Read the story to find out.

[1] ***inning:*** one part of a baseball game (A baseball game has nine innings.)

BASEBALL FEVER

At baseball stadiums in Japan, there is a tradition: During the seventh inning of every baseball game, the people in the stadium stand up and sing the fight song of their team. Then, all together, the fans release long, colorful balloons.

At baseball stadiums in the United States, the crowd stands up and sings during the seventh inning, too. But they don't sing their team's fight song. At every stadium, in every city, they sing the same song: "Take Me Out to the Ball Game." Almost everyone knows the words to the song by heart.

There is a story behind that tradition, and the story begins over 100 years ago.

In the spring of 1908, a young man named Jack Norworth was riding a train in New York City when he saw a sign that said "BASEBALL GAME TODAY." Jack was a songwriter, and those three words gave him an idea for a song. He took out a piece of paper and began writing a song about Katie Casey, a young woman who loved baseball. Fifteen minutes later, the words to the song were finished.

The song "Take Me Out to the Ball Game" was a huge hit in 1908, and it remained popular for many years. But as time went by, the song became less well-known. At some baseball stadiums, a musician sometimes played the song on an organ. But the organist played only the verse that begins "Take me out to the ball game," and the crowd never sang along.

A man named Harry Caray made the song popular again in 1976. Harry was the announcer at a baseball stadium in Chicago. His job was to describe the game for people who watched it on TV. During the seventh-inning stretch,[1] he loved to sing along when the organist played "Take Me Out to the Ball Game." The microphone was off then, so the crowd couldn't hear him sing.

One day Harry's boss walked by and heard Harry singing. "You should turn on the microphone," his boss said. "Maybe everybody will sing with you."

"But I don't have a good voice!" Harry said.

"I know," his boss said. "That's why you should sing! The crowd will probably sing with you because they'll think, 'If *he* can sing, so can I.'"

A few days later, Harry turned the microphone on and sang "Take Me Out to the Ball Game" during the seventh-inning stretch. The crowd sang with him, and a tradition was born. The tradition spread from Chicago to other cities in the United States. Then it spread to other cities in the world. But as the tradition moved around the world, it changed; in other countries, fans sang different songs and added their own traditions. Who knows? Maybe the tradition will circle the world and come back to Chicago. Maybe next year, fans there will sing "Take Me Out to the Ball Game" and then, all together, they will release long, colorful balloons into the sky.

---

[1] ***the seventh-inning stretch:*** a time when people in baseball stadiums stand up, stretch their arms and legs, and sometimes walk around

③ VOCABULARY

Which words have the same meaning as the words in *italics*? Write the letter of your answer on the line.

1. __e__ Baseball stadiums have seventh-inning *customs*.

2. _____ People *open their hands and let* the balloons *go into the air*.

3. _____ The crowd knows the words *from memory*.

4. _____ The song was a *very big* hit.

5. _____ It *stayed* popular for many years.

6. _____ It was *famous*.

a. by heart
b. huge
c. remained
d. well-known
e. traditions
f. release

4 COMPREHENSION

◆ **Understanding the Main Ideas**

There are two correct ways to complete each sentence. Circle the letters of the *two* correct answers.

1. During the seventh inning of baseball games in Japan, fans
   a. release colorful balloons.
   b. give presents to their favorite players.
   c. sing their team's fight song.

2. During the seventh inning of baseball games in the United States, fans
   a. blow horns.
   b. sing "Take Me Out to the Ball Game."
   c. stand up and stretch.

3. Jack Norworth wrote the song "Take Me Out to the Ball Game"
   a. on a train in New York City.
   b. in 15 minutes.
   c. for a company that sold peanuts.

4. The song "Take Me Out to the Ball Game"
   a. was a huge hit in 1908.
   b. remained popular for many years.
   c. is about a baseball player named Jack Casey.

5. The tradition of singing during the seventh inning began
   a. at a baseball stadium in Chicago.
   b. in several U.S. cities at the same time.
   c. with an announcer named Harry Caray.

6. As the tradition moved around the world, fans in other countries
   a. added their own traditions.
   b. sang different songs.
   c. added verses to the song "Take Me Out to the Ball Game."

◆ **Understanding Adjective Clauses**

Find the best way to complete each sentence. Write the letter of your answer on the line.

1. Jack Norworth saw a sign __e__

2. Katie Casey was a young woman ____

3. Organists played only the verse ____

4. Harry Caray was an announcer ____

5. He described the game for people ____

a. who loved baseball.

b. that begins "Take me out to the ball game."

c. who worked at a baseball stadium in Chicago.

d. who watched it on TV.

e. that said "BASEBALL GAME TODAY."

◆ Understanding Time and Place

Read the phrases from the story. Which phrases tell you *when* something happened?
Write them in the *WHEN* column. Which phrases tell you *where* something happened?
Write them in the *WHERE* column.

- 15 minutes later
- in New York City
- during the seventh inning
- in Chicago

- around the world
- in the spring of 1908
- at baseball stadiums in Japan
- a few days later

WHEN	WHERE
15 minutes later	

5 DISCUSSION/WRITING

Baseball games usually last two or three hours. (That is why fans stand up and stretch
during the seventh inning!) Because baseball games can be slow, some people think that
baseball is boring.

**Together with the class, make a list of exciting sports to watch. Your teacher will write
the list on the board. Complete the two sentences below. Then share your writing in a
small group.**

1. I think the sport of _____ is exciting to watch because
_____.

2. I think the sport of _____ is boring to watch because
_____.

1 PRE-READING

Look at the picture.

➤ When is this?

➤ What kind of uniform are the people wearing?

➤ The player on the right is a woman. How old is she? What is she going to do? How does she feel?

➤ How do the two men feel?

2 READING

In the last story, you read that the song "Take Me Out to the Ball Game" was about a young woman named Katie Casey. Katie loved to watch baseball. The next story is also about a woman who loved baseball. But she didn't love to *watch* it; she loved to *play* it. Did she have success as a baseball player?

Read the story to find out.

THREE STRIKES—AND THE PITCHER'S OUT?

When Jackie Mitchell was born in 1914, she weighed only three and a half pounds.[1] Her parents worried about her because she was tiny. To help her grow up strong and healthy, they made sure she got plenty of exercise.

When Jackie was six, her father taught her how to play baseball. He loved the sport, and she did, too. They spent hours in their yard throwing a ball back and forth.

The Mitchells' neighbor was a professional baseball player. His name was Dizzy Vance, and he was a pitcher. One day he watched Jackie play baseball with her father.

"You have a strong arm," Dizzy told Jackie. "Do you want me to show you how to pitch?"

"Sure!" Jackie said.

Dizzy threw a special pitch called a drop pitch: The ball came to the plate in a straight line and then suddenly dropped. Dizzy taught Jackie how to throw a drop pitch. By the time she was eight, she was really good at it.

Jackie played on girls' baseball teams until she was 17 years old. Then she signed a contract to play on a minor-league[2] men's team in Tennessee called the Lookouts. She was the only woman in the United States who played on a men's team.

On April 2, 1931, the New York Yankees came to Tennessee to play the Lookouts. The game was just for fun, but 4,000 people came to watch it. The Yankees had two powerful hitters—Babe Ruth and Lou Gehrig. People wanted to see Jackie pitch to them.

When it was Babe Ruth's turn to bat, he tipped his cap to Jackie to be polite. Then he got ready to hit the ball. Jackie threw a drop pitch. Babe swung[3] and missed. "Strike!" the umpire called. Jackie threw another drop pitch. Babe swung and missed that one, too—another strike. Babe didn't swing at the third pitch, but it went across the plate. That was strike three, and Babe Ruth was out. He threw his bat down and walked angrily away from the plate.

Lou Gehrig was the next batter. He swung at three pitches—and missed them all. He was out. The crowd went wild.

A few days later, Jackie received a letter from the baseball commissioner.[4] He wrote that he had canceled Jackie's contract with the Lookouts because baseball was "too strenuous" for a woman. Jackie was off the team.

For the next several years, Jackie played baseball with some small teams. But their games were not really games—they were mostly shows. In one game, Jackie pitched while sitting on a donkey. After that game, she quit baseball. She returned to her hometown, got a job, and later married. She never played baseball again.

In 1931, before the game against the Yankees, Jackie told a reporter, "Maybe I will be the first woman to pitch in the big leagues." She never got that chance. But it wasn't because she wasn't good enough. Maybe it was because she was *too* good.

---

[1] **three and a half pounds:** 1.6 kg. [2] **minor-league:** a group of teams that play against one another (Most minor-league teams are in small cities.) [3] **swung:** the past tense of *swing* (Batters swing the bat when they try to hit the ball.) [4] **baseball commissioner:** the person who makes the big decisions in professional baseball

3 **VOCABULARY**

Match the words with the people and things in the picture. Write the number of your answer on the line.

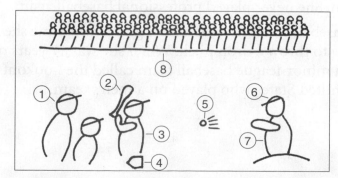

  7 **a.** pitcher   **e.** umpire

      b. bat   **f.** batter

      c. plate   **g.** pitch

      d. cap   **h.** fans

COMPREHENSION

◆ **Understanding the Main Ideas**

Imagine that a reporter interviewed Jackie Mitchell when Jackie was an old woman. Below are the reporter's questions. Write Jackie's answers on the lines.

1. Who taught you how to pitch?

   Dizzy Vance taught me. He was a neighbor who was a professional baseball player.

2. What is a drop pitch? Can you explain it, please?

   _____

3. How many people came to watch the Lookouts play the Yankees?

   _____

4. Why did people come to watch the game?

   _____

5. What did Babe Ruth do after the umpire called, "Strike three"?

   _____

6. Why did the baseball commissioner cancel your contract with the Lookouts?

   _____

7. What did you do after you quit baseball?

   _____

◆ **Understanding a Summary**

Imagine this: You want to tell the story "Three Strikes—And the Pitcher's Out?" to a friend. You want to tell the story quickly, in only four sentences. Which four sentences tell the story best? Check (✔) your answer.

a. ☐ Jackie Mitchell was a pitcher for a minor-league baseball team called the Lookouts. In 1931, she pitched against two of the most powerful hitters in baseball, and both men were out on strikes. After the game, the baseball commissioner canceled Jackie's contract, and she was off the team. She never played professional baseball again.

b. ☐ Jackie Mitchell learned to play baseball when she was a little girl. By the time she was eight years old, she knew how to throw a drop pitch. When she was 17 years old, she signed a contract to play for a minor-league baseball team called the Lookouts. She was the only woman in the United States who played on a men's team.

◆ Finding Information

Read each question. Find the answer in the paragraph below and circle it. Write the number of the question above the answer.

1. When was Jackie Mitchell born?

2. How much did she weigh?

3. Why were her parents worried about her?

4. What did they do to help her grow up strong and healthy?

5. How old was Jackie when she learned how to play baseball?

6. Who taught her?

7. Where did they practice?

When Jackie Mitchell was born (in 1914), she weighed only three and a half pounds. Her parents worried about her because she was tiny. To help her grow up strong and healthy, they made sure she got plenty of exercise.

When Jackie was six, her father taught her how to play baseball. They spent hours in their yard throwing a ball back and forth.

5 DISCUSSION/WRITING

In 1931, the baseball commissioner canceled Jackie Mitchell's contract because he thought the game of baseball was "too strenuous" for a woman.

The young woman in the photo is Eri Yoshida. She is a pitcher who wants to play major-league baseball in the United States. What do you think? Is it a good idea for women to play with men on professional baseball teams?

Check (✔) your opinion. (Check only one sentence.)
Then, on the lines below the sentences, explain your answer.

a. ☐ It is OK for women to play baseball with men.

b. ☐ It is not OK for women to play baseball with men.

_____

_____

_____

UNIT 3 SOMEBODY TO LEAN ON

THE SONG

- The title of the song is "Lean on Me." Discuss the meaning of the expression *lean on* with the class.

- Close your book and listen to the song. As you listen, write some of the words and phrases you understand on your own paper. Then share your words with the class. What do you think the song is about?

- Now open your book and listen to the song again. Read the words as you listen.

LEAN ON ME

Sometimes in our lives,
We all have pain,
We all have sorrow.
But if we are wise,
We know that there's
Always tomorrow.

Lean on me when you're not strong,
And I'll be your friend.
I'll help you carry on.
For[1] it won't be long
'Til[2] I'm gonna[3] need
Somebody to lean on.

Please swallow your pride
If I have things
You need to borrow.
For no one can fill
Those of your needs
That you won't let show.

You just call on me, brother, when you
   need a hand.
We all need somebody to lean on.
I just might have a problem that you'll
   understand.
We all need somebody to lean on.

Lean on me when you're not strong,
And I'll be your friend.
I'll help you carry on.
For it won't be long
'Til I'm gonna need
Somebody to lean on.

You just call on me, brother, when you
   need a hand.
We all need somebody to lean on.
I just might have a problem that you'll
   understand.
We all need somebody to lean on.

If there is a load
You have to bear
That you can't carry,
I'm right up the road.
I'll share your load
If you just call me.

Call me (if you need a friend) . . .

- **Listen to the song again. Lip-sync[4] the words as you listen.**

---

[1] **For:** because
[2] **'Til:** until
[3] **gonna:** going to
[4] **Lip-sync:** to pretend you are singing—to move your lips, but not speak; pronounced "lip-sink"

1 PRE-READING

Look at the picture.

➤ Where is this man?

➤ How does he feel?

2 READING

Bill Withers wrote the song "Lean on Me." The song is about people that he knew. Who were those people?

Read the story to find out.

A HUSBAND AND FATHER TO LEAN ON

Bill Withers grew up in the small town of Slab Fork, West Virginia. In Slab Fork, almost all the men were miners, and almost all the families were poor.

The people in Bill's hometown didn't have much money, but they had one another to lean on. If anyone needed a hand doing some work, someone helped. If anyone needed to talk over a problem, someone listened. If anyone needed to borrow a tool or a cup of sugar, someone lent it. For example, Bill's family had a telephone but not a refrigerator. The neighbors across the road had a refrigerator but not a telephone. When Bill's family needed ice, they walked across the road and got it from the neighbors. When those neighbors needed to make a phone call, they walked across the road and used the phone at Bill's house.

Bill's father died when Bill was 13—a lot of miners died young—and his family became even poorer. So when he was 17, Bill left home to join the U.S. Navy. He didn't want to work in the mines, and the navy gave him his best chance at a better life. The navy trained him as a mechanic, and for nine years he traveled around the world on navy ships. In his free time, he wrote songs. His friends told him his songs were good.

After Bill got out of the navy, he moved to Los Angeles and got a job in an airplane factory. In his free time, he continued to write songs. He bought a small electric piano, and he liked to run his fingers up and down the keys. Sometimes he found the melody for a song that way.

One day in 1972, Bill was sitting at the piano when he got an idea for a song. "Lean on me," he sang as he played. "It's a good beginning," Bill thought. "But how should the song continue? What are some examples of people helping one another? Where do people lean on one another? In Los Angeles? No. In Los Angeles, a man can die on the side of the freeway and it's eight days before anybody notices."

Bill began to think about his hometown, Slab Fork. He remembered all the borrowing and lending; the talking and listening; the working and helping. *That* was a place where people leaned on one another. When Bill thought about Slab Fork, he knew how to continue the song. A long time ago, the people there had shown him how.

The song "Lean on Me" was a big hit. Bill wrote other hit songs, too, and he became a famous musician. But in 1985, he suddenly quit the music business: He stopped performing, and he stopped writing songs. Why? He had a wife and two children—a boy and a girl—and he wanted to be near them. He knew how difficult it was to grow up without a father. He didn't want to be in a recording studio or on a stage in a faraway city when his children needed him. He gave up fame—and a lot of money—to be a husband and father his family could always lean on.

3 VOCABULARY

Complete the sentences with the words below.

a hand	faraway	~~grew up~~	melody	quit

1. Bill Withers lives in California now, but he _____ grew up _____ in West Virginia.

2. Anyone in Slab Fork who needed _____ got help.

3. A song needs words and a _____.

4. Bill stopped performing, and he _____ writing songs, too.

5. Bill wanted to be near his family, not on a _____ stage.

COMPREHENSION

◆ **Understanding the Main Ideas**

Complete the sentences. Write your answers on the lines.

1. Bill Withers grew up in a big city, right?

   No, he didn't. He _grew up in a small town_____.

2. Almost all the men in Slab Fork were farmers, right?

   No, they weren't. They _____.

3. Almost all the families were rich, right?

   No, they weren't. They _____.

4. People there leaned on the government, right?

   No, they didn't. They _____.

5. Bill left home to join a rock band, right?

   No, he didn't. He _____.

6. He wrote short stories in his free time, right?

   No, he didn't. He _____.

7. "Lean on me" was a good ending for a song, right?

   No, it wasn't. It _____.

8. The song is about the people in Los Angeles, right?

   No, it isn't. It _____.

◆ **Understanding Cause and Effect**

Find the best way to complete each sentence. Write the letter of your answer
on the line.

1. Bill's family walked across the road for
   ice __b__

2. When he was 13, Bill's family became
   even poorer ____

3. He joined the U.S. Navy ____

4. He liked to run his fingers up and
   down the piano keys ____

5. He gave up fame and money ____

a. because he wanted to be near his
   wife and children.

b. because the neighbors had a
   refrigerator.

c. because his father died.

d. because he didn't want to work in
   the mines.

e. because sometimes he found the
   melody for a song that way.

◆ **Understanding Time Sequence**

Match the events and the dates. Copy the sentences in the correct order.

He wrote the hit song "Lean on Me."
He joined the U.S. Navy.
He quit the music business.
He moved to Los Angeles.
~~Bill Withers was born in Slab Fork, West Virginia.~~

1. 1938 _Bill Withers was born in Slab Fork, West Virginia._____

2. 1955 _____

3. 1967 _____

4. 1972 _____

5. 1985 _____

5 DISCUSSION/WRITING

A. In the song "Lean on Me," Bill Withers wrote, "No one can fill . . . needs that you won't let show."

What do you need? Make a list. Here is what one student wrote.

a map of the bus routes
a photo for my student ID
ideas for an inexpensive weekend trip
a new cell phone

Now write your list here.

_____

_____

_____

_____

B. Read your list in a small group. Listen carefully when your classmates read their lists. If you have information that might help your classmates, share it.

STORY 6

1 PRE-READING

Look at the picture.

➤ Where are the women?

➤ How do they feel?

➤ Why are they hugging?

2 READING

In the last story, you read about Bill Withers, who wrote "Lean on Me." The song is about the people in the small town of Slab Fork, West Virginia. The two women in the next story were not from a small town—they were from a big city—and they didn't know each other well. But one of the women helped the other in an important way. How did she help?

Read the story to find out.

A CUP OF COFFEE AND A KIDNEY TO GO

Every morning for three years, Annamarie Ausnes stopped on her way to work in Tacoma, Washington, to buy a cup of coffee. She loved coffee, so she went to a coffee shop where each cup was made fresh. She always arrived at 8:15, and she always ordered the same thing: a small coffee to go. That was her morning routine.

Another part of her morning routine was talking to Sandra Andersen, the coffee shop employee who made her coffee. Their conversation was mostly small talk—they talked about their grandchildren, the weather, and their vacations. They never saw each other outside the coffee shop, and they didn't even know each other's name. But they both enjoyed their short conversations. Annamarie was always smiling and cheerful. She was one of Sandra's favorite customers.

One morning when Annamarie walked into the coffee shop, Sandra knew immediately that something was wrong. Annamarie wasn't smiling, and she didn't seem to want to talk.

"Are you OK?" Sandra asked.

Annamarie didn't answer for a few seconds. Then she said, "Actually, no."

"What's wrong?" Sandra asked.

"I have kidney disease," Annamarie answered. "It's no surprise—doctors told me that 20 years ago. But now it's worse, and I need a kidney transplant."

"Can anyone in your family donate a kidney?" Sandra asked as the line of customers behind Annamarie grew longer.

"No," Annamarie answered. "My husband and my son got tested, but they weren't good matches."

"I'll get tested," Sandra said immediately.

Annamarie was shocked. Was the woman who made her morning coffee willing to give her one of her kidneys?

Yes, she was. Sandra asked Annamarie to give her the information she needed to get tested. A few days later, she went to the hospital for a blood test. She found out that she and Annamarie were a match. She also found out that donating a kidney was not easy. "You'll be in the hospital for a week," a doctor told her, "and you can't go back to work for six weeks. It'll be another six months before you're really back to normal."

"I want to do it," Sandra said. Later, she told her husband that she wanted to donate a kidney to one of her customers. They talked it over, and he said it was OK with him.

The next time Annamarie came to the coffee shop, Sandra reached across the counter and took her hand. "I'm a match," she told Annamarie. The women held hands and cried.

When Sandra arrived at the hospital to donate her kidney, Annamarie was waiting for her at the door. She gave Sandra a red rose. Then the two women checked into the hospital for their surgeries. Both operations went well. Six weeks later, the women were ready to go back to work.

The evening before Sandra returned to work at the coffee shop, her husband told her, "You saved Annamarie's life, and that's special—*you're* special." Then he laughed a little. "But if someone walks into the coffee shop and says they don't feel good, please don't give away another body part!"

③ VOCABULARY

Show you understand the meaning of the words in *italics*. Read each sentence. If it is correct, circle *YES*. If it is not correct, circle *NO*.

1. If something is part of your *routine*, you do it often.   (YES)   NO

2. A sky that is *mostly* cloudy has a lot of clouds.   YES   NO

3. *Small talk* is a serious conversation.   YES   NO

4. If you want to *transplant* something, you have to move it.   YES   NO

5. If you *donate* something, you are paid for it.   YES   NO

6. Things that *match* are similar in some way.   YES   NO

4 COMPREHENSION

◆ **Understanding the Main Ideas**

Circle the letter of the correct answer.

1. Annamarie and Sandra were
   a. close friends who met every day for coffee.
   b. a customer and an employee at a coffee shop.
   c. doctors at a hospital in Tacoma, Washington.

2. When Annamarie told Sandra she needed a kidney transplant, Sandra said,
   a. "I'll get tested."
   b. "I'll help you find a donor."
   c. "That's not an easy operation."

3. The blood test showed that Sandra
   a. had kidney disease, too.
   b. could not donate a kidney.
   c. was a match for Annamarie.

4. Today Sandra
   a. still works at the coffee shop, but only three hours a day.
   b. asks all her customers about their health.
   c. has only one kidney but feels fine.

◆ **Finding More Information**

Read each sentence on the left. Which sentence on the right gives you more information? Write the letter of the answer on the line.

1. __c__ Annamarie was always smiling and cheerful.

2. ____ Sandra knew that something was wrong.

3. ____ Annamarie's kidney disease was no surprise.

4. ____ Annamarie's husband and son couldn't donate a kidney.

5. ____ The operations went well.

a. They weren't good matches.
b. The women were back at work six weeks later.
c. She was one of Sandra's favorite customers.
d. Doctors had told her about it 20 years ago.
e. Annamarie wasn't smiling, and she didn't seem to want to talk.

◆ **Understanding Dialog**

Below is the conversation between Annamarie and Sandra. Some words are missing from their conversation. Write the missing words on the lines. Then practice the conversation with a partner. One student is speaker A, and the other student is speaker B.

A: Are you OK?

B: _____Actually_____, no.

A: What's wrong?

B: I have kidney _____. Doctors told me that 20 years ago. But now it's

_____, and I need a kidney _____.

A: Can anyone in your family _____ a kidney?

B: No. My husband and my _____ got tested, but they weren't good

matches.

A: I'll get _____.

5 DISCUSSION/WRITING

Annamarie and Sandra's conversations were mostly small talk. The topics of their conversations were their grandchildren, the weather, and their vacations.

A. What are some good topics for small talk? With your classmates, make a list on the board.

B. What are some good opportunities to make small talk in English? Share your ideas with the class.

C. With a partner, write a conversation of small talk. Write your conversation on the lines below. One person is speaker A, and the other person is speaker B. Practice your conversation several times with your partner. If you would like to, say your conversation for the class.

A: _____

B: _____

A: _____

B: _____

A: _____

B: _____

A: _____

B: _____

UNIT 4

A SIMPLE LIFE

THE SONG

- Close your book and listen to the song. As you listen, draw pictures, shapes, or lines; write words; or write nothing at all. Then share your drawing or writing with a partner. (If you didn't draw or write anything at all, tell your partner why you didn't.) How did the song make you feel? Tell your partner.

- The word 'tis means "it is." What do you think 'twill and 'til mean? Of those three words, which one do people still use today?

- Now open your book and listen to the song again. Read the words as you listen.

SIMPLE GIFTS

'Tis the gift to be simple, 'tis the gift to be free.
'Tis the gift to come down where you ought to be.
And when we find ourselves in the place just right,
'Twill be in the valley of love and delight.
When true simplicity is gained,
To bow and to bend we will not be ashamed.
To turn, turn will be our delight,
'Til by turning, turning, we come round right.

And when we find ourselves in the place just right,
'Twill be in the valley of love and delight.
When true simplicity is gained,
To bow and to bend we will not be ashamed.
To turn, turn will be our delight,
'Til by turning, turning, we come round right.

- **Listen to the song again. As you listen, complete the phrases below.
  Write the letter of your answer on the line. (You will write some letters twice.)**

1. 'Tis the gift to be simple, **'**tis the gift to
   be __e__

2. 'Tis the gift to come down where you
   ought to ____

3. And when we find ourselves in the
   place just ____

4. 'Twill be in the valley of love and ____

5. When true simplicity is ____

6. To bow and to bend we will not
   be ____

7. To turn, turn will be our ____

8. 'Til by turning, turning we come
   round ____

a. ashamed
b. be
c. delight
d. right
e. free
f. gained

STORY 7

1 PRE-READING

Look at the picture.

➤ How old is this man?

➤ Where does he live?

➤ What kind of work does he do?

2 READING

The song "Simple Gifts" comes from a religious group called the Shakers. Who are the Shakers? Where do they live? What do they believe?

Read the story to find out.

THE LAST THREE?

Arnold Hadd is 60 years old and lives on a beautiful farm in Maine. Every morning he gets up early and starts to work. There's a lot of work to do: The farm has an apple orchard, a large vegetable garden, and hayfields. There are sheep, cows, and pigs to take care of, too. Arnold works hard all morning and then takes a break. For half an hour, he and the other people on the farm pray and sing some religious songs together. Then they eat a big hot meal. After lunch, Arnold gets back to work, and he doesn't stop until dinner at six.

Arnold has lived on the farm for more than 30 years, but the farm is not his. The farm makes money, but Arnold never gets a paycheck. He has a "family," but he has no wife or children. Arnold is a Shaker.

The Shakers are a religious group that came to the United States from England in 1774. They are called Shakers because they used to dance and move during their religious services. That has changed; Shakers do not do that anymore. But the rules Shakers live by have not changed for hundreds of years. They are:

1. Live communally. Shakers do not own property. When people become Shakers, they give everything they have to the group. After they join, they must ask the group for permission to buy something—a new coat or a new tool, for example—and the group gives them money to buy it.
2. Live simply. Shakers do not buy anything they don't really need to survive, like video games or jewelry.
3. Live in peace with your neighbors. Shakers do not fight in wars or carry guns.
4. Men and women must live separately. Shaker men and women live in the same building, but on separate sides, and they use separate staircases and doors. They sit apart when they pray and eat. No children are born into the Shaker religion. The only way to become a Shaker is to join the group as an adult.

Shakers live by the motto "Hands to work, hearts to God." They believe that it is important to work hard. They are famous for the beautiful furniture they make. It is simple, but the quality is excellent.

The Shakers are also famous for the song "Simple Gifts," which a Shaker minister wrote in 1848. Shakers still sing the song during their religious services. It is popular with other people in the United States, too. Musicians played it at the inauguration of President Barack Obama in 2009.

In the 1800s, there were 6,000 Shakers in the United States. They lived in 19 Shaker communities. Today there is only one Shaker community left; it is the farm where Arnold Hadd lives. Sometimes people who are thinking about becoming Shakers visit the farm. Arnold shows them around and explains the rules that Shakers live by. Every year about ten people come, but so far, not one person has joined the group. Only three Shakers live on the farm—Arnold Hadd and two elderly women. They are perhaps the last Shakers on earth.

3 VOCABULARY

Complete the sentences with the words below.

communally	elderly	inauguration	orchard

1. The farm has an _____ with more than 100 apple trees.

2. A Shaker does not own a car or a house because Shakers live _____.

3. When Barack Obama became president, musicians played "Simple Gifts" at his _____.

4. Two _____ women live on the farm. They are both more than 80 years old.

4 COMPREHENSION

◆ Remembering Details

Which sentences describe Arnold Hadd? Check (✔) five answers. (The first one is done for you.)

☑ He is 60 years old.	☐ He works hard every day.
☐ He has three children.	☐ He gets a big paycheck every week.
☐ He lives on a farm in Maine.	☐ He is a Shaker.
☐ He gets up early every morning.	☐ He owns a lot of property.

◆ Finding Information

Read each question. Find the answer in the paragraph below and circle it. Write the number of the question above the circled answer.

1. How many Shakers were in the United States in the 1800s?

2. How many Shaker communities did they live in?

3. How many Shaker communities are left?

4. Where is it?

5. What do people who are thinking about becoming Shakers do?

6. Who shows them around?

7. What does he explain?

8. How many people come every year?

9. How many people have joined the group so far?

10. How many Shakers live on the farm?

       In the 1800s, there were (6,000) Shakers in the United States. They lived in 19 Shaker communities. Today there is only one Shaker community left; it is a farm in Maine. Sometimes people who are thinking about becoming Shakers visit the farm. Arnold Hadd shows them around and explains the rules that Shakers live by. Every year about ten people come, but so far, not one person has joined the group. Only three Shakers live on the farm—Arnold Hadd and two elderly women. They are perhaps the last Shakers on earth.

◆ Checking Facts

Read the sentences about Shaker life. If the information is correct, put a check (✔) under *YES*. If the information is not correct, put a check under *NO*. If the information is not in the story, put a check under *NOT IN STORY*.

	YES	NO	NOT IN STORY
1. Shakers play video games.	☐	☑	☐
2. They give everything they have to the group.	☐	☐	☐
3. The women wear jewelry.	☐	☐	☐
4. The women wear dark blue dresses.	☐	☐	☐
5. The men and women live separately.	☐	☐	☐
6. They make furniture.	☐	☐	☐
7. They fight in wars.	☐	☐	☐
8. They don't work on Sundays.	☐	☐	☐
9. They carry guns.	☐	☐	☐
10. They sing "Simple Gifts" during their religious services.	☐	☐	☐

5 DISCUSSION/WRITING

Some rules that Shakers live by are: Live communally, live simply, and live in peace with your neighbors.

A. What are two rules to live by—rules that all children should know? Write the rules on the lines below.

1. _____

2. _____

B. Now share your rules with your classmates. Follow these steps.

1. Walk around the room. Tell your two rules to a classmate. Listen to your classmate's two rules. Memorize *one* of your classmate's rules, and add it to your two rules.

2. Continue to walk around the room. Tell another classmate your three rules (your two rules, plus the one you added). Listen to your classmate's three rules. Memorize *one* of your classmate's rules, and add it to your three rules.

3. Continue to walk around the classroom. Tell another classmate your four rules.

4. Take a seat and share a rule that you especially like with the class.

STORY 8

1 PRE-READING

Look at the picture.

➤ What are the three young men going to do?

➤ Do you have any experience with this sport?

➤ Do you want to try it?

➤ Is it popular in your native country?

2 READING

In the last story, you read about the Shakers, who believe that it is "a gift to be simple." You also read the rules the Shakers live by. The next story is about a family who lived a simple life. What kind of simple life did they live? What rules did they live by?

Read the story to find out.

A WONDERFUL GIFT?

In the summer of 1957, Dorian Paskowitz was surfing up and down the coast of California. One day he stopped for lunch at a small café. There he met his future wife. Her name was Juliette, and she was tall—over six feet—with black hair and brown eyes. She was an opera singer. Dorian was a blue-eyed, suntanned surfer. It was love at first sight for both of them.

A few months after they met, Dorian told Juliette, "I want to marry you, but there's something I need to tell you. I was trained as a doctor, but I don't want to be a doctor. I want to be a surfer. So I'll never have much money."

"That's OK," Juliette said. "I don't care about money."

"There's more," Dorian continued. "I want to have a big family, but I don't want our children to go to school. We'll live in a camper and travel all over the world. We'll go from beach to beach, and the children will learn to surf. The world will be their classroom, and we'll be their teachers."

Juliette thought it over for a few minutes. "Yes," she said. "I'll marry you."

Dorian and Juliette got married, bought a camper, and began their unusual life together. During the next 16 years, they had nine children—eight boys and one girl. The family lived by these rules:

1. Live simply and have only what you need to survive. The Paskowitzes' camper was small—only 24 feet long. The only girl had her own bed, but the boys slept like puppies, three or four to a bed. Their only clothes were underwear, T-shirts, and shorts, and they usually went barefoot. They had books, but they had no TV and no toys. When the family needed money, Dorian worked as a doctor. He never worked for long because the family lived on very little money.

2. Eat simply. Dorian didn't allow his children to eat any fat or sugar because he thought it was unhealthy. So the children never had candy, soft drinks, or fast food. Every morning they ate a special breakfast that Juliette made. It was a mix of berries and whole grains. The children said it looked like food for birds, but they ate it.

3. Surf whenever possible. The family surfed all over the world—in Egypt, Israel, Venezuela, Hawaii, Mexico, and the United States. All of the children were excellent surfers, and some became world champions.

The Paskowitz children are grown now, with families of their own. What do they think about their unusual childhood? They have mixed feelings. Navah, the only daughter, says, "Our parents didn't give us an education, and that was unfair. But I'll never forget the exciting experiences we had." Moses, the fifth son, says, "It was really crowded in our camper. But with seven brothers, I always had a best friend."

Joshua, the youngest child, says, "We never got presents on our birthdays. Our father took us to the water and said, 'For your birthday, I give you the sea.' When I was a child, I thought, 'Why can't we get presents like other kids?' But now I think he gave us a wonderful gift."

3 VOCABULARY

Complete the sentences with the words below.

| allow | barefoot | fast food | thought it over | ~~trained~~ |

1. Dorian went to medical school. He was _____trained_____ as a doctor.

2. When Dorian told Juliette his plan for their family, she didn't speak for a few minutes. She _____.

3. Sometimes the children wore shoes, but usually they went _____.

4. The children never ate hamburgers because their father didn't _____ them to eat _____.

4 COMPREHENSION

◆ **Understanding the Main Ideas**

Complete the sentences. Write your answers on the lines.

1. Did Dorian and Juliette meet in Hawaii?

   No, they didn't. They _met in California_____.

2. Did they meet in 1977?

   No, they didn't. They _____.

3. Was Juliette a nurse?

   No, she wasn't. She _____.

4. Did Dorian and Juliette have four children?

   No, they didn't. They _____.

5. Did they live in a house?

   No, they didn't. They _____.

6. Did they travel only in the United States?

   No, they didn't. They _____.

7. When the family needed money, did Dorian work as a teacher?

   No, he didn't. He _____.

8. Do the children have only good feelings about their unusual childhood?

   No, they don't. They _____.

◆ **Understanding Contrasts**

Find the best way to complete each sentence. Write the letter of your answer
on the line.

1. Dorian was trained as a doctor, __c__

2. He wanted to have a big family, ____

3. The children had books, ____

4. Navah didn't have an education, ____

5. Moses says it was crowded in the camper, ____

6. The children never got birthday presents, ____

a. but they had no TV and no toys.

b. but she had exciting experiences.

c. but he wanted to be a surfer.

d. but they had the gift of the sea.

e. but he always had a best friend.

f. but he didn't want his children to go to school.

◆ Understanding a Summary

Imagine this: You want to tell the story "A Wonderful Gift?" to a friend. You want to tell the story quickly, in only five sentences. Which five sentences tell the story best? Check (✔) your answer.

a. ☐ The nine Paskowitz children had an unusual childhood. They had a simple life, without TV and without toys, and they ate a simple diet. They didn't live in a house—they lived in a small camper—and they didn't go to school. They traveled all over the world and learned to surf. Today they have mixed feelings about their unusual childhood.

b. ☐ In the summer of 1957, Dorian Paskowitz was surfing in California when he walked into a small café and met a woman named Juliette. It was love at first sight for both of them. Dorian was trained as a doctor, but he didn't want to work as a doctor; he just wanted to surf. He asked Juliette to marry him, and she said yes. They got married and had nine children.

5 DISCUSSION/WRITING

A. What do you think of the way Dorian and Juliette Paskowitz chose to live? The sentences below describe their family. Read each sentence and put a check (✔) under *GOOD IDEA, NOT A GOOD IDEA,* or *I'M NOT SURE*.

	GOOD IDEA	NOT A GOOD IDEA	I'M NOT SURE
1. They had nine children.	☐	☐	☐
2. They lived in a small camper.	☐	☐	☐
3. They traveled all over the world.	☐	☐	☐
4. The children didn't go to school.	☐	☐	☐
5. The children had no TV.	☐	☐	☐
6. The children had no toys.	☐	☐	☐
7. The children never ate candy.	☐	☐	☐
8. The children never ate fast food.	☐	☐	☐

B. On your own paper, explain *one* of your answers above. Then share your writing in a small group. Here is what one student wrote.

The children didn't go to school. I think it's not a good idea. Children need to learn about the world, their country's history, math, science, etc. I don't think most parents know enough about all those things.

UNIT 5 THE WAY TO PEACE

THE SONG

- The title of the song is "Peace Train." Is there peace in your native country now? Tell the class.

- Close your book and listen to the song. Just for fun, count how many times you hear the words *peace train*. Then look in the Answer Key to see if you counted correctly.

- Now open your book and listen to the song again. Read the words as you listen.

PEACE TRAIN

Now I've been happy lately, thinking
  about the good things to come.
And I believe it could be, something
  good has begun.

Oh, I've been smiling lately, dreaming
  about the world as one.
And I believe it could be, someday it's
  going to come.

'Cause[1] out on the edge of darkness,
  there rides a peace train.
Oh, peace train, take this country, come
  take me home again.

Now I've been smiling lately, thinking
  about the good things to come.
And I believe it could be, something
  good has begun.

Oh, peace train sounding louder.
Glide on the peace train.
Come on the peace train,

Yes, peace train holy roller.
Everyone, jump upon the peace train.
Come on the peace train.

Get your bags together, go bring your
  good friends, too
'Cause it's getting nearer, it soon will be
  with you.

Now come and join the living, it's not so
  far from you,
And it's getting nearer, soon it will all be
  true.

Oh, peace train sounding louder.
Glide on the peace train.
Come on the peace train.

Now I've been crying lately, thinking
  about the world as it is.
Why must we go on hating, why can't
  we live in bliss?

'Cause out on the edge of darkness,
  there rides a peace train.
Oh, peace train, take this country, come
  take me home again.

Oh, peace train sounding louder.
Glide on the peace train.
Come on the peace train.

Yes, peace train holy roller.
Everyone, jump upon the peace train.
Come on, peace train.
Yes, it's the peace train.
Come on the peace train, oh, peace
  train.

- **The singer is happy because he is "thinking about the good things to come." What good things are coming in your life? (It can be something big, like a wedding, or something small, like the cup of tea you are going to drink after class.) First, make a list of three things and share your list with a partner. Next, choose one thing, write it on a piece of paper, and tape your paper to the board. Finally, listen to the song again while you read your classmates' papers.**

---

[1] **'Cause**: because

1 PRE-READING

Look at the picture.

➤ Where do you think the women in the photo live?

➤ What are they doing?

➤ How do you think they feel?

2 READING

The songwriter who wrote "Peace Train" sang the song at a concert in honor of the man in the next story. Who is the man? What honor did he receive? Why did he receive the honor?

Read the story to find out.

THE PROFESSOR AND THE PEACE TRAIN

In 1976, Muhammad Yunus was a young professor at a university in Bangladesh. One day he went for a walk in Jobra, a nearby village. The people in Jobra were very, very poor.

A woman was sitting in front of a small house. She was making a stool out of bamboo.

"That's a beautiful stool," he said. "Where do you get the bamboo?"

"I buy it," she answered.

"How much does it cost?" Professor Yunus asked. He taught economics, so he was interested in the woman's business.

"It costs five taka,"[1] she answered. That was about 22 cents in U.S. money.

"Do you have five taka?"

"Oh, no. I borrow it from the *paikars*."

"The *paikars*? The middlemen?"

"Yes," the woman explained. "A middleman gives me five taka to buy the bamboo. I make a stool and then, at the end of the day, I sell the stool to the middleman for five taka and 50 poisha."[2]

"So your profit is only 50 poisha for each stool?" That was two cents in U.S. money.

"Yes," she answered and went back to work.

The professor couldn't stop thinking about the woman. She made only two cents for a day's work! Later he found out that 42 people in Jobra were borrowing money from the middlemen because banks didn't lend money to poor people.

The professor took some cash out of his own pocket, returned to the village, and gave the money to the 42 people. "Buy your materials and make your products," he told them. "Then sell them at the market, not to the middlemen. Pay me back whenever you can." Every one of the 42 people paid Professor Yunus back.

The professor began lending money to poor people in other villages, too. Five years later, he was lending money to people in 100 villages. "They won't pay you back," bankers warned him. But every person paid him back, with interest. He knew then that it was possible to have a bank just for the poor. In 1983, he opened Grameen Bank.

In the Bangla language, *grameen* means "village." Professor Yunus chose the name because the first people who borrowed money lived in villages in Bangladesh. Today the Grameen Bank lends money to poor people all over the world, in small villages like Jobra and in big cities like Chicago. Every year the bank lends more than $750 million, almost all of it in very small loans.

In 2006, Muhammad Yunus received the Nobel Peace Prize. There was a concert in his honor, and the songwriter who wrote "Peace Train" sang the song. Before he sang, he said, "We can have peace only if we end poverty, and Muhammad Yunus is trying to end poverty."

That is the dream of Muhammad Yunus and the Grameen Bank: to end poverty, one small loan at a time.

---

[1] **taka:** pronounced TAH-kuh [2] **poisha:** pronounced POY-shuh (There are 100 poisha in one taka.)

3 VOCABULARY

Complete the sentences with the words below.

lend	materials	profit	whenever

1. If you buy something for $5 and sell it for $8, your _____ is $3.

2. If you want to borrow money, you have to find someone who will _____ it to you.

3. If you want to make something, you have to have the necessary _____.

4. If someone tells you, "Come at any time," you can come _____ you want to.

4 COMPREHENSION

◆ **Understanding the Main Ideas**

Complete the sentences. Write your answers on the lines.

1. Where was Muhammad Yunus working in 1976?

    He was working at a university in _____Bangladesh_____.

2. What did he teach?

    He taught _____.

3. Where did he go for a walk one day?

    He went for a walk in Jobra, a nearby _____.

4. Why did the people in Jobra borrow money from the middlemen?

    Banks didn't lend money to _____ people.

5. Where did Professor Yunus get the money he lent to the people in Jobra?

    He took the money out of his own _____.

6. Where did he tell the people to sell their products?

    He told them to sell their products at the _____.

7. How big are the loans the Grameen Bank makes?

    Almost all of them are very _____.

8. What prize did Professor Yunus receive in 2006?

    He received the Nobel _____ Prize.

◆ **Understanding a Summary**

Imagine this: You want to tell the story "The Professor and the Peace Train" to a friend. You want to tell the story quickly, in only four sentences. Which four sentences tell the story best? Check (✔) your answer.

a. ☐ In 1976, Muhammad Yunus was a professor at a university in Bangladesh. He taught economics, so he was interested in the businesses in a nearby village. Every time he visited the village, he couldn't stop thinking about the people who lived there. He often lent small amounts of money to them.

b. ☐ In 1976, Muhammad Yunus began to make small loans to poor people in villages in Bangladesh. He lent the money to them because banks didn't lend money to poor people. That was the beginning of the Grameen Bank. Today the bank lends money to poor people all over the world.

◆ Understanding Dialog

Below is the conversation between Professor Yunus and the woman who was making a stool. Some words are missing from their conversation. Write the missing words on the lines. Then practice the conversation with a partner. One student is speaker A, and the other student is speaker B.

A: That's a _____ beautiful _____ stool. Where do you get the _____?

B: I _____ it.

A: How much does it cost?

B: It _____ five taka.

A: Do you have five taka?

B: Oh, no. I _____ it from the *paikars*.

A: The *paikars*? The middlemen?

B: Yes. At the _____ of the day, I sell the stool to a middleman for five taka and 50 poisha.

A: So your _____ is only 50 poisha for each stool?

B: Yes.

5 DISCUSSION/WRITING

In 2006, Muhammad Yunus received the Nobel Peace Prize. Imagine this: You are going to give someone a prize.

In the center of the medal below, write the name of the prize. (For example, you can write *Best Cook* or *Best Friend*.) Complete the two sentences next to the medal and read them to a partner. Then tell your partner more about the person you want to honor with a prize.

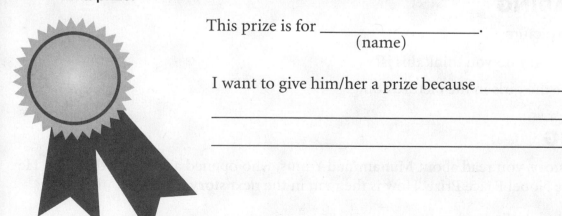

This prize is for _____.

(name)

I want to give him/her a prize because _____

_____

_____.

1 PRE-READING

Look at the picture.

➤ What country do you think this is?

➤ What are the girls in the picture doing?

2 READING

In the last story, you read about Muhammad Yunus, who opened a bank for the poor. He received the Nobel Peace Prize. How is the man in the next story trying to build peace?

Read the story to find out.

THREE CUPS OF TEA

In 1993, Greg Mortenson tried to climb K2, the second highest mountain in the world. He didn't succeed. Only 600 meters from the top, a man in his climbing group became sick. Greg helped the man down the mountain, to a place where a helicopter could land. After that, Greg was exhausted. He decided to walk down the mountain. On the way down, he got lost.

Greg walked alone for days and nearly froze to death. At last, he came to a village. A wrinkled old man greeted him with these words: "Peace be with you." The man's name was Haji Ali, and the village was Korphe, in Pakistan. Haji Ali was the village chief.

For the next several weeks, Haji Ali took care of Greg. Greg slept at his house, in a place of honor near the fire, and he ate the meals that Haji Ali's wife prepared for him. Every day Greg got stronger.

One morning Haji Ali took Greg for a walk around Korphe. They came to some open land where 84 children sat on the ground. The children were using sticks to write in the dirt. "We don't have a school building," Haji Ali explained, "so the children practice their lessons here."

Greg put his hands on Haji Ali's shoulders and made a promise: "I will build a school in Korphe."

Greg went home to the United States, got a job, and began to save money. He figured he needed about $12,000 for the school. "It will take me a long time to save $12,000," he thought.

A man named Jean Hoerni heard about Greg's plan to build a school in Korphe. Jean was a rich man, and he was also a mountain climber. He sent Greg a check for $12,000. "Build the school," he told Greg. "When it's finished, bring me a picture of it."

Greg returned to Korphe with supplies to build the school, and construction began. Greg was at the construction site from sunrise to sunset. He was trying to make the work go faster.

One day Haji Ali tapped Greg on the shoulder. "Greg," he said, "you are doing a lot for my people. But you must do one more thing for me."

"Anything," Greg said.

"Sit down and shut your mouth. You're making everyone crazy." He gave Greg a cup of tea. "You must respect our ways. The first time you share tea with us, you are a stranger. The second time, you are a friend. The third time, you are family." He put his hand on Greg's hand. "You must take time to share three cups of tea."

The school was finished in 1996, three years after Greg Mortenson walked into Korphe as a stranger. He brought a photo of the school to Jean Hoerni, who was very pleased. He gave Greg $1 million to build more schools.

Greg Mortenson says that Haji Ali was the wisest man he ever knew. "We Americans think we have to do everything quickly," he says. "But Haji Ali taught me to slow down and share three cups of tea. Building things is important, but building relationships is important, too. It is really the only way to peace."

3 VOCABULARY

Which words have the same meaning as the words in *italics*? Write the letter of your answer on the line.

1. __f__ After he helped the sick man, Greg was *very tired*.

2. ____ Greg *almost* died.

3. ____ Haji Ali *spoke to Greg and welcomed* him.

4. ____ He was the *leader* of the village.

5. ____ Haji Ali *touched Greg* on the shoulder *with his hand*.

6. ____ Jean Hoerni was *happy* when he saw the photo of the school.

a. greeted
b. chief
c. tapped
d. pleased
e. nearly
f. exhausted

4 COMPREHENSION

◆ Understanding Details

Read the summary of the story "Three Cups of Tea." There are 13 mistakes in the summary. Find the mistakes and cross them out. Write the correct words. (The first one is done for you.)

<u>1993</u>
In ~~1983~~, Greg Mortenson tried to climb K2, the third highest mountain in the world. He didn't succeed. Only 6 meters from the top, a woman in his climbing group got sick, and Greg helped her down the mountain. After that, he was exhausted and decided to walk up the mountain.

He walked alone for weeks. At last, he came to a village named Korphe, in Afghanistan. He stayed with an old man named Haji Ali. Greg discovered that Korphe didn't have a hospital. "I will return and build one," he told Haji Ali.

A rich man named Jean Hoerni gave Greg $120,000 to build the school. Greg returned to Korphe with supplies, and construction on the school began. While he was in Korphe, Greg learned a lot from Haji Ali, who was the oldest man he ever knew.

The school was finished in 1996, four years after Greg walked into Korphe as a stranger. Jean Hoerni was pleased with the school and gave Greg $5 million to build more schools.

◆ Understanding Word Groups

Read each group of words. One word in each group doesn't belong. Find the word and cross it out.

climb	build	first	school
mountain	supplies	five	children
~~helicopter~~	write	third	meters
high	construction site	second	lessons

◆ **Finding More Information**

Read each sentence on the left. Which sentence on the right gives you more information? Write the letter of your answer on the line. (The sentences on the right are not in the story, but they are true.)

1. __f__ K2 is the second highest mountain in the world.

2. ____ Greg nearly froze to death.

3. ____ A wrinkled old man greeted him.

4. ____ Haji Ali's wife prepared food for Greg.

5. ____ Greg got a job.

6. ____ The Korphe school was finished in 1996.

7. ____ Jean Hoerni gave Greg $1 million to build more schools.

a. Almost everyone in the village helped build it, including the children.

b. During the next ten years, Greg built sixty schools.

c. He worked as a nurse at a hospital in San Francisco.

d. When he woke up one morning, ice covered his nose and mouth.

e. He had a gray beard and wore a hat made of lambswool.

f. Most mountain climbers believe it is the most difficult mountain to climb.

g. She often gave him a drink made with yogurt and a flat bread called *chapatti*.

5 DISCUSSION/WRITING

When Greg arrived in Korphe, Haji Ali invited him into his house. He gave Greg a seat of honor near the fire. Then he gave him some dried meat and a cup of tea. Greg didn't like the meat, but he ate it to be polite. In your native country, how do you welcome people into your home? When you are a guest in someone's home, what do you do to be polite?

Find two ways to finish each sentence below. Then share your writing with a partner.

1. When a guest comes to our home, we . . .

   • _____.

   • _____.

2. When I am a guest in someone's home, I . . .

   • _____.

   • _____.

UNIT 6 YOU CAN'T JUDGE A BOOK BY ITS COVER

THE SONG

- Close your book and listen to the song "I Dreamed a Dream." Just for fun, count how many times you hear the words *dream, dreams,* and *dreamed*. Then look in the Answer Key to see if you counted correctly.

- The word *dream* has two meanings. (Think, for example, about these two sentences: *My dream is to open a small store. I had a wonderful dream last night.*) Discuss the two meanings of *dream* with your teacher and the class. What does the word mean in this song?

- Now open your book and listen to the song again. Read the words as you listen.

I DREAMED A DREAM

I dreamed a dream in time gone by,
When hope was high and life worth living.
I dreamed that love would never die.
I prayed that God would be forgiving.

Then I was young and unafraid,
And dreams were made and used and wasted.
There was no ransom to be paid,
No song unsung, no wine untasted.

But the tigers come at night
With their voices soft as thunder,
As they tear your hopes apart
And they turn your dream to shame.

And still I dreamed he'd come to me,
That we would live the years together.
But there are dreams that cannot be,
And there are storms we cannot weather.

I had a dream my life would be
So different from this hell I'm living,
So different now from what it seemed.
Now life has killed the dream I dreamed.

- **Listen to the song again. As you listen, notice the words that rhyme
(for example, *by* and *die*; *living* and *forgiving*). One verse has no
words that rhyme. Which verse is it?**

1 PRE-READING

Look at the picture.

➤ The woman in the photo is famous. Do you know why she is famous? If you do, tell the class.

➤ If you don't know why this woman is famous, take a guess.

2 READING

The song "I Dreamed a Dream" is from the musical *Les Miserables*, which is about the difficult lives of people who lived in France in the 1800s. *Les Miserables* is a popular musical. There are translations in 21 languages, and people all over the world go to see it. In 2009, the woman in the photo made the song "I Dreamed a Dream" *really* popular. How did she do that? How did the song make *her* really popular, too?

Read the story to find out.

SUSAN'S GOT TALENT

For the first 47 years of her life, Susan Boyle lived quietly in a village in Scotland. But on April 11, 2009, she became one of the most famous people in the world.

On that day, Susan Boyle was a contestant on a talent show in Britain. When she walked onto the stage, some people in the audience laughed a little. Susan was short, plump, and middle-aged. She had frizzy gray hair, and she was wearing a gold dress that she had bought for a nephew's wedding.

"How old are you?" one of the judges asked her.

"I'm 47," she answered.

"Wow," the judge said. "OK, what's the dream?"

"I'm trying to be a professional singer," Susan replied. The audience shook their heads and laughed.

"And why hasn't that worked out for you so far?" the judge asked.

"I never had a chance before," Susan explained. "But here's hoping it will change." Susan told the three judges she was going to sing the song "I Dreamed a Dream," and the music began to play. Susan looked at the audience, smiled, and began to sing. She had a beautiful voice! Within seconds, the audience was applauding and cheering. Within minutes, they were on their feet. Even one of the judges was standing and clapping.

When Susan finished singing, the judges said that her performance was incredible. "You can go back to your village with your head held high," they told her. "It's three yeses!" Susan shook her fists in the air and did a little dance. Then she blew a kiss to the audience and walked off the stage.

That night Susan's performance was on the Internet. Within nine days, people had watched it 100 million times. People everywhere loved Susan. They loved her even more when they learned more about her.

Susan was the youngest of ten children. When she was born, she didn't get enough oxygen. Doctors told her parents, "Susan has some brain damage. It will probably be difficult for her to learn."

The doctors were right: It was difficult for Susan to learn, and the children at school teased and bullied her. Although learning was difficult for Susan, singing was easy. Whenever she felt sad or lonely, she sang.

The years went by. Susan tried several times to become a professional singer, but it didn't work out for her. Her father died, and then her mother became old and sick. Susan took care of her mother for years, until she died in 2007. When Susan sang, "I had a dream my life would be so different," was she singing about her own life? Many people thought so.

After Susan sang, one of the judges told her, "That was the biggest surprise I have had in three years of this show. I'm in shock." Susan's performance surprised everyone: the judges, the audience, and the millions of people who watched it on the Internet. Maybe the only person who wasn't surprised was Susan. Before she sang, she said, "I've always wanted to perform in front of a large audience. I'm going to make that audience rock."[1] Susan did more than rock the audience. She rocked the world.

---

[1] **I'm going to make that audience rock:** I'm going to get the audience excited.

3 VOCABULARY

Complete the sentences with the words below.

although	bullied	clapping	shock

1. The audience was applauding; even one of the judges was _____.

2. Susan's performance was surprising. One judge said he was in _____.

3. When Susan was born, her brain was damaged, but her voice was not. So _____ learning was difficult, singing was easy.

4. Sometimes Susan was afraid at school because children _____ her.

COMPREHENSION

◆ **Understanding the Main Ideas**

Complete the sentences. Write your answers on the lines.

1. Where did Susan Boyle live?

   She lived in a ___village in Scotland___.

2. When was the talent show?

   It was on _____.

3. What happened to Susan on that day?

   She became one of the most _____ people in the world.

4. What did Susan look like?

   She was short, plump, and _____, with

   frizzy _____ hair.

5. How old was she?

   She was _____.

6. What was Susan's dream?

   She wanted to be a _____.

7. What did the judges say about Susan's performance?

   They said it was _____.

8. Within nine days, how many times had people watched Susan's performance on the Internet?

   People had watched it _____.

◆ **Understanding Word Groups**

Read each group of words. One word in each group doesn't belong. Find the word and cross it out.

talent show	audience	short	clap	help	but
contestant	fist	plump	reply	tease	although
~~village~~	performance	middle-aged	cheer	bully	and
judges	stage	surprised	applaud	laugh at	wow

◆ **Remembering Details**

People loved Susan Boyle even more when they learned more about her. What did they learn? Check (✔) seven sentences. (The first one is done for you.)

☑ She was the youngest of ten children.

☐ When she was born, she didn't get enough oxygen.

☐ She didn't talk until she was four years old.

☐ It was difficult for her to learn.

☐ She went to a special school for children with learning difficulties.

☐ The children at school teased and bullied her.

☐ Whenever she felt sad or lonely, she sang.

☐ She played the guitar and the violin.

☐ She tried to become a professional singer several times.

☐ She took care of her mother for years.

5 DISCUSSION/WRITING

A. In the next exercise, you will learn more about your classmates, and they will learn more about you.

Follow these steps.

1. On your own paper, write three sentences about yourself. Write information that is probably new to your classmates. For example:

   - I am a good dancer.
   - I have three sisters.
   - Yesterday I bought a new TV.

2. Walk around the room and find a partner. Tell your partner your sentences, and listen carefully to your partner's sentences. Then repeat the activity two more times with new partners.

3. Take your seat and, on your own paper, write what you learned about your classmates. Write as many sentences as you can. Then share the information with the class.

B. After Susan Boyle's performance, many people said, "You can't judge a book by its cover." Discuss the meaning of that saying with your classmates. Do you have a similar saying in your native language? If so, share it with the class.

STORY 12

1 PRE-READING

Look at the picture.

➤ Where is this man from?

➤ What kind of work does he do?

➤ How does he feel?

2 READING

In the last story, you read about Susan Boyle, who surprised people with her singing. What is surprising about the man in the photo?

Read the story to find out.

THE KING IN THE NURSING HOME

For 22 years, Charles Mumbere worked as a nurse's aide in the United States. He worked in nursing homes, where he took care of elderly people. He helped his patients take baths, get dressed, and eat. He pushed their wheelchairs, and he held their arms when they walked. All those years, no one—not his patients, not his supervisors, not his coworkers—knew that in his native country, Charles Mumbere was a king.

Charles was from the African country of Uganda. In Uganda, there were several kingdoms. His father was the leader of a kingdom called Rwenzururu. After his father died, Charles became king at age 18. When Charles was 32, the Ugandan government sent him to the United States to study English and business. He went to a school in Washington, D.C., and the Ugandan government paid all his expenses. But three years after Charles arrived in the United States, there was a sudden change in government in Uganda. The new government did not recognize Rwenzururu as a kingdom, and it immediately stopped sending Charles money.

Overnight Charles's life changed. One day, he was a king and a student. The next day, he was a man with no money and no job. Charles needed to find work fast. He decided to get training as a nurse's aide. "There will always be sick people, and there will always be old people," he thought. "I won't make much money as a nurse's aide, but I'll always find work."

Charles was right. As soon as he finished his training, he got a job as a nurse's aide. During the next 22 years, he worked at several nursing homes. Charles enjoyed his work—he liked helping people. But it was not the life he had dreamed of when he was young. He never stopped thinking about Rwenzururu, and he never stopped wanting to go back.

Finally, there was another change in government in Uganda. The new government recognized Rwenzururu as a kingdom and Charles Mumbere as its leader. So in 2009, Charles returned to Uganda. In a big celebration with dancing and drumming, Charles again became King of Rwenzururu.

For the second time, Charles's life changed overnight. In the United States, he lived in a small apartment. Now he lives in a large house. When he worked as a nurse's aide, he wore a cotton uniform every day. Now he wears a suit, and for special ceremonies, he wears a green robe. In the United States, nobody knew that Charles was an important man in his native country. In Rwenzururu people know he is important. Security guards are around him 24 hours a day.

Charles's life has changed, but Charles himself has not. During all those years as a nurse's aide, he worked hard. Now he is working hard in Rwenzururu. Many houses do not have running water, and the roads are not good. Most of the people are poor farmers. For 22 years, Charles took good care of his patients. There are 300,000 people in Rwenzururu. Now Charles is trying to take good care of them.

3 VOCABULARY

Circle the word or words that correctly complete the sentence.

1. A nurse's *aide* helps / teaches a nurse.

2. People who live in *nursing homes* are usually young / old.

3. Someone who is 50 / 80 is *elderly*.

4. People who have *coworkers* work alone / with other people.

5. People who have *expenses* need medicine / money.

6. People who want to get *training* usually go to a school / station.

4 COMPREHENSION

◆ Understanding the Main Ideas

Circle the letter of the correct answer.

1. When Charles Mumbere was in the United States, who knew that he was a king?
   a. Only his supervisors and coworkers knew.
   b. Only his patients knew.
   c. No one knew.

2. Why did Charles come to the United States?
   a. He wanted to study English and business.
   b. He wanted to ask for money for Rwenzururu.
   c. He wanted to learn about building roads.

3. Who paid Charles's expenses?
   a. His father sent him money.
   b. The Ugandan government sent him money.
   c. The U.S. government gave him money.

4. Why did Charles get training as a nurse's aide?
   a. He had studied medicine in his native country.
   b. His uncle owned a nursing home.
   c. He thought, "I'll always find work."

5. Why did Charles return to Uganda in 2009?
   a. The U.S. government told him he had to leave.
   b. He couldn't find work in the United States.
   c. The new Ugandan government recognized him as the king of Rwenzururu.

6. What is *not* a problem in Rwenzururu?
   a. There is a danger of earthquakes.
   b. Many houses do not have running water.
   c. The roads are not good.

◆ Understanding Time Relationships

Find the best way to complete each sentence. Write the letter of your answer on the line.

1. Charles became king __b__
2. He went to the United States ____
3. Charles was suddenly without money ____
4. Charles worked as a nurse's aide ____
5. Charles returned to Uganda ____

a. three years after he arrived in the United States.
b. when he was 18.
c. in 2009.
d. for 22 years.
e. when he was 32.

◆ Understanding Contrasts

Which people, places, and things were part of Charles's life in the United States? Which people, places, and things are part of his life in Rwenzururu? Put a check (✔) under *U.S.* or *RWENZURURU*.

	U.S.	RWENZURURU
1. a green robe	☐	☑
2. a small apartment	☐	☐
3. patients	☐	☐
4. security guards	☐	☐
5. supervisors	☐	☐
6. a large house	☐	☐
7. a suit	☐	☐
8. a nursing home	☐	☐
9. coworkers	☐	☐

5 DISCUSSION/WRITING

Charles Mumbere's life in Rwenzururu is very different from his life in the United States. For example, in the United States, he lived in a small apartment, but now he lives in a big house. Are you living in a new country? How is your life different?

On the lines below, write two sentences about the differences between your life in your native country and your life now. Connect the two parts of each sentence with the word *but*. Then read your sentences to a partner. For example:

In Mexico I walked everywhere, but now I drive everywhere.
In Kosovo I was a professor, but now I am a factory worker.

1. _____

2. _____

UNIT 7 GREAT ESCAPES

THE SONG

- Look at the picture of the stars. The name of this group of stars in English is the Big Dipper. What is its name in your native language? What does that mean in English? How can people who travel at night use these stars to find their way?

- To the right is a picture of two drinking gourds. What is a gourd? If you know, tell the class. Then close your book and listen to the song. Just for fun, count the number of times you hear the words *follow the drinking gourd*. Then look in the Answer Key to see if you counted correctly.

- Now open your book and listen to the song again. Read the words as you listen.

FOLLOW THE DRINKING GOURD

Follow the drinking gourd.
Follow the drinking gourd
For[1] the old man is coming
Just to carry you to freedom.
Follow the drinking gourd.

When the sun comes back
And the first quail[2] calls,
Follow the drinking gourd
For the old man is waiting
Just to carry you to freedom.
Follow the drinking gourd.

Follow the drinking gourd.
Follow the drinking gourd
For the old man is waiting
To carry you to freedom.
Follow the drinking gourd.

Well, the riverbank makes a mighty
  good road.
Dead trees will show you the way,
Left foot, peg foot traveling on.
Follow the drinking gourd.

Follow the drinking gourd.
Follow the drinking gourd
For the old man is waiting
To carry you to freedom.
Follow the drinking gourd.

Well, the river ends between two hills.
Follow the drinking gourd.
There's another river on the other side.
Follow the drinking gourd.

Follow the drinking gourd.
Follow the drinking gourd
For the old man is waiting
To carry you to freedom.
Follow the drinking gourd.

Well, where the great big river meets
  the little river,
Follow the drinking gourd.
The old man is waiting to carry you to
  freedom.
Follow the drinking gourd.

Follow the drinking gourd.
Follow the drinking gourd
For the old man is waiting
To carry you to freedom.
Follow the drinking gourd.

For the old man is waiting
Just to carry you to freedom
If you follow the drinking gourd.

- After you read the story on page 65, return to this page and listen to the song again.

---

[1] **For:** because
[2] **quail:** a bird (People sometimes eat it.)

STORY 13

1 PRE-READING

Look at the picture and the map.

➤ How old is the picture?

➤ Where are the men from?

➤ Why are there holes in the man's pants?

➤ The map shows the United States in 1860. How were the light gray states different from the dark gray states? Tell the class what you know.

2 READING

The song "Follow the Drinking Gourd" helped people escape. What did they escape from? How did the song help them escape?

Read the story to find out.

THE DRINKING GOURD

In 1860, 4 million people in the United States were slaves. They were from Africa—or they were the children of people from Africa—and they lived in the South. Most of them worked in cotton and sugar fields on farms called plantations.

An old man named Peg-leg Joe worked on the plantations. People called him Peg-leg Joe because the bottom of his right leg was missing. At the end of that leg, there was a peg—a short piece of wood. Joe walked on his good left leg and on the peg leg. Peg-leg Joe traveled from plantation to plantation and did small jobs. He was not a slave; plantation owners paid him for his work.

In the evenings, Peg-leg Joe sang with the slaves on the plantations. He sang one song over and over until the slaves could sing it, too. The song was "Follow the Drinking Gourd." Why did he sing that song? Peg-leg Joe helped slaves escape to the North, where there was no slavery. The song gave them directions.

The song began: "When the sun comes back . . ." That meant: "Wait until spring to escape, when the weather in the North is warmer."

It continued: "Follow the drinking gourd." A gourd is a vegetable with a hard shell. Slaves used gourds as drinking cups. What did that mean: "Follow the drinking gourd"? One group of stars in the night sky is the Big Dipper. It is called the Big Dipper because the stars look like a cup that people dip into water. Two of the stars in the Big Dipper point to the North Star. "Follow the drinking gourd" meant: "Look up at the Big Dipper. Walk toward the North Star."

The song told slaves, "Dead trees will show you the way—left foot, peg foot." What did that mean? Peg-leg Joe drew a left foot and a big dot on some trees. The drawings showed slaves the way to the North.

Finally, the song told slaves to travel along the rivers. Small rivers took them to big rivers until they reached the Ohio River, which separated the North from the South. The "old man"—Peg-leg Joe—waited there to help them cross the Ohio River. On the other side of the river, the slaves were free.

The story of Peg-leg Joe and his song is amazing. But is it true? Was there really a man named Peg-leg Joe? Did the song "Follow the Drinking Gourd" give slaves directions? Historians aren't sure. Many don't think so. But this *is* true: People sometimes helped slaves escape; escaped slaves often traveled along rivers; and escaped slaves followed the North Star. Most important, it is true that many slaves escaped. In 1865, slavery ended all over the United States. Before that time, over 100,000 slaves followed the drinking gourd to freedom.

3 VOCABULARY

Match the words and their meanings. Write the letter of your answer on the line.

1. __c__ plantation
2. ____ peg
3. ____ over and over
4. ____ gourd
5. ____ amazing
6. ____ historian
7. ____ all over

a. many times
b. so surprising that it is difficult to believe
c. a large farm in a hot country
d. a vegetable with a hard shell
e. everywhere
f. a short piece of wood
g. someone who studies history

4 COMPREHENSION

◆ Understanding the Main Ideas

Circle the letter of the correct answer.

1. This is a story about a song that
   a. was popular in the 1860s.
   b. helped slaves escape.
   c. slaves sang while they worked.

2. Peg-leg Joe was a man who
   a. escaped to freedom.
   b. owned a plantation.
   c. helped slaves escape.

◆ Remembering Details

A. Which sentences describe most slaves in the United States in the 1860s? Check (✔) four answers. (The first one is done for you.)

☑ They were from Africa or were the children of people from Africa.

☐ They could read and write English.

☐ They lived in the South.

☐ They lived on plantations.

☐ Plantation owners paid them for their work.

☐ They worked in cotton and sugar fields.

B. Which sentences describe Peg-leg Joe? Check (✔) four answers.

☐ He was old.

☐ He was the son of a slave.

☐ He did small jobs on the plantations.

☐ Part of one leg was missing.

☐ In the evenings, he sang with the slaves.

☐ He was from Canada.

◆ Checking Facts

Read each sentence below. Do historians think it is true? Put a check (✔) under *TRUE* or *NOT SURE*.

	TRUE	NOT SURE
1. Over 100,000 slaves escaped.	☐	☐
2. People sometimes helped slaves escape.	☐	☐
3. The song "Follow the Drinking Gourd" helped slaves escape.	☐	☐
4. Escaped slaves traveled along rivers.	☐	☐
5. Escaped slaves followed the North Star.	☐	☐
6. There was a man named Peg-leg Joe.	☐	☐

5 DISCUSSION/WRITING

Was there really a man named Peg-leg Joe? Historians aren't sure. But they *are* sure about the woman in the photo. Her name was Harriet Tubman. She was an escaped slave who returned to the South 13 times and helped 70 slaves escape.

Who is someone who helped (or helps) a lot of people? (It can be someone famous, or it can be someone you know.) On the lines below, write a few sentences about him or her. Then share your writing with a partner. Here is what one student wrote about one of her English teachers.

Jorge Islas-Martinez helps a lot of people in our community. He helps them learn English, and he also helps them know their rights. He translates for them at the hospital and in court. People call him when they have a problem. We are so lucky to have Jorge.

_____

_____

_____

_____

1 PRE-READING

Look at the picture and the map.

➤ What kind of balloon do you see in the picture?

➤ Where is the balloon? (What are some possible countries?)

➤ Look at the map to the right. It is a map of Germany, 1945–1989. How was East Germany different from West Germany? Tell the class what you know.

2 READING

In the last story, you read about slaves in the United States who followed the Big Dipper to escape to the North. That story is from 1860. The next story is from 1979. It is about another group of people who wanted to escape. Where did they live? Why did they want to escape? Where did they want to go?

Read the story to find out.

TWELVE KILOMETERS TO A NEW LIFE

In 1979, Peter Strelzyk and his friend Günter Wetzel lived in East Germany. Both men were unhappy in East Germany because they didn't like the government. They wanted to move to West Germany with their families. That was impossible. There was a wall between East and West Germany, and East Germans weren't allowed to travel to the West. But Peter had a plan.

"I think I can fly my wife and two sons over the wall in a hot-air balloon," Peter told Günter.

"In a hot-air balloon?" Günter asked. "Are you serious?"

"Yes, I think I can make one," Peter said. "I'll buy fabric, cut it into big triangles, and sew the pieces together to make a balloon. I'll make a passenger basket out of wood." Peter began to talk faster. "We'll take the balloon to a meadow in the woods. Then I'll use propane gas to heat the air in the balloon, and we'll take off. From the meadow, it's only 12 kilometers[1] to West Germany—a 30-minute balloon ride."

Peter bought 850 meters[2] of fabric, and Günter helped him cut and sew it. A month later, the balloon was finished.

In the middle of the night, Peter and his family took off in the balloon. Everything was fine for the first 20 minutes. Then the balloon went into a cloud. The fabric became wet and heavy, and the balloon slowly came down.

After the balloon landed, the family got out of the passenger basket and looked around. Ahead of them, they saw the wall. "Did we fly over it in the dark?" they wondered. "Are we in West Germany?" Peter saw a plastic bread bag on the ground. He picked it up and read the words on the bag: "People's Bakery, Wernigerode." His heart sank. Wernigerode was a town in East Germany. The balloon had landed in East Germany, only 500 meters[3] from the wall. The family left the balloon and went home.

The next day, they decided there was only one thing to do: make another balloon and try again.

"I'll help you make a bigger balloon," Günter told Peter. "The next time you leave, my family and I are going with you."

The two men bought more fabric, but this time they had to be extra careful. The East German police had found the balloon and were looking for the people who had made it. Peter, Günter, and their wives went to dozens of stores and bought only a few meters of fabric at a time. When they had enough fabric, the two men sewed as fast as they could; some days they sewed for 16 hours. When the second balloon was finished, the two families—four adults and four children—took off. The balloon went up into the air, flew for 30 minutes, and slowly came down. Everyone got out of the passenger basket and looked around. Were they in West Germany? They weren't sure.

"Are we in the West?" they asked a man.

"You're in Bavaria," the man said.

The two families shouted with joy. Bavaria was a state in West Germany. They were on the other side of the wall.

---

[1] **12 kilometers:** 7.5 miles   [2] **850 meters:** 930 yards   [3] **500 meters:** 546 yards

3 VOCABULARY

Circle the word or words that correctly complete the sentence.

1. If something is *allowed*, it is OK / not OK to do it.

2. You use *fabric* to make clothes / machines.

3. A *triangle* looks like this: ▭ / △.

4. A *meadow* usually has a lot of trees / grass.

5. *Propane gas* is for cooking and heating / cars and airplanes.

6. The *middle of the night* is about 2 A.M. / 5 A.M.

7. The number of things in a *dozen* is 12 / 20.

4 COMPREHENSION

◆ **Reviewing the Story**

Write the missing words on the lines.

In 1979, there was a _____wall_____ between East and West Germany, and East
                                    1.
Germans were not allowed to travel to the _____. Peter Strelzyk, an East
                                                          2.
German, wanted to live in West Germany. He decided to take his family over the wall in a
hot-air _____. With the help of his friend Günter, he made a balloon out
              3.
of pieces of _____.
                        4.

The Strelzyk family didn't make it to West Germany on their first try. The balloon
went into a _____, got wet, and came down too soon. It landed in East
                        5.
Germany, only 500 _____ from the wall.
                              6.

Peter and Günter made a second balloon, and both families _____
                                                                              7.
off in it. That time, the balloon landed in West Germany, on the other
_____ of the wall.
        8.

◆ **Remembering Details**

What did Peter plan to do? Check (✔) seven answers. (The first one is done for you.)

Peter planned to . . .

☑ buy fabric.

☐ cut the fabric into big triangles.

☐ sew the pieces together to make a balloon.

☐ ask his mother to help him sew.

☐ make a passenger basket out of wood.

☐ hide the balloon in a neighbor's garage.

☐ take the balloon to a meadow.

☐ heat the air in the balloon with propane gas.

☐ take off on a cloudy day.

☐ fly over the wall.

◆ Finding More Information

Read each sentence on the left. Which sentence on the right gives you more information? Write the letter of your answer on the line.

1. __b__ It was impossible to travel from East Germany to West Germany.

2. _____ From the meadow, it was only 12 kilometers to West Germany.

3. _____ Peter saw a plastic bag.

4. _____ Peter and Günter had to be extra careful.

5. _____ They sewed as fast as they could.

6. _____ The balloon landed in Bavaria.

a. Some days they sewed for 16 hours.
b. There was a wall between the two countries.
c. It was a state in West Germany.
d. He read the words on it: "People's Bakery, Wernigerode."
e. That was a 30-minute balloon ride.
f. The East German police were looking for them.

5 DISCUSSION/WRITING

A. Imagine that you have a hot-air balloon that can take you anywhere you want to go. Where do you want it to take you? Complete the sentences below. Then share your sentences with a partner.

I want the balloon to take me to _____.

I want to go there because _____.

B. On your own paper, answer the questions below in complete sentences. Then share your sentences with a partner.

1. Peter and his family left East Germany in 1979. When did you leave your native country?

2. Peter wanted to leave East Germany because he didn't like the government there. Why did you leave your country?

3. It was difficult for Peter to leave because he wasn't allowed to travel to the West. Was it difficult for you to leave? If so, explain why.

4. Peter and his family traveled by balloon. How did you travel?

5. The balloon ride to West Germany was 30 minutes long. How long was your trip?

6. Peter and his family felt happy when they arrived in West Germany. How did you feel when you arrived in a new country? Why did you feel that way?

UNIT 8 SURVIVORS

THE SONG

- Close your book and listen to the song. As you listen, draw pictures, shapes, or lines; write words; or write nothing at all. Then share your drawing or writing with a partner. (If you didn't write anything at all, tell your partner why you didn't.) How did the song make you feel? Tell your partner.

- The song is the theme to the movie *Titanic*. Was the song popular in your native country? Was the movie popular in your native country? Tell the class.

- Now open your book and listen to the song again. Read the words as you listen.

MY HEART WILL GO ON

Every night in my dreams,
I see you, I feel you.
That is how I know you go on.

Far across the distance
And spaces between us,
You have come to show you go on.

Near, far, wherever you are,
I believe that the heart does go on.
Once more you open the door,
And you're here in my heart
And my heart will go on and on.

Love can touch us one time
And last for a lifetime
And never let go 'til[1] we're gone.

Love was when I loved you
One true time I hold to.
In my life, we'll always go on.

Near, far, wherever you are,
I believe that the heart does go on.
Once more you open the door,
And you're here in my heart
And my heart will go on and on.

You're here, there's nothing I fear,
And I know that my heart will go on.
We'll stay forever this way.
You are safe in my heart,
And my heart will go on and on.

- **Listen to the song again. In a small group, write a dictation.
  Follow these steps.**

1. Read the four short verses of the song (the verses that begin "Every night," "Far across," "Love can," and "Love was"). Be sure you understand all the words and can spell them.

2. Your teacher will assign your group one of the verses. Close your book and listen to the song. As you listen, write your group's verse on your own paper.

3. When the class has finished listening to the entire song, show your writing to the people in your group. Together, decide on one version of the verse to write on the board.

4. Listen to the song again. Was your group's writing correct?

---

[1] **'til:** until

1 PRE-READING

Look at the picture.

➤ The ship in the picture is the *Titanic*. Tell the class what you know about it.

2 READING

"My Heart Will Go On" is the theme song to the movie *Titanic*. The stars of the movie helped the woman in the next story. How did they help her?

Read the story to find out.

THE LITTLEST PASSENGER

On April 10, 1912, the Dean family—Bertram, Eva, and their two small children—got on a ship in England. They were going to travel to New York because Bertram hoped to open a small shop in the United States. It was the beginning of a new life for them.

The name of the ship was *Titanic*, and this was its first voyage. The *Titanic* was the world's largest ship; it carried more than 2,000 passengers. The first-class passengers traveled in luxury. For them, the ship had a swimming pool, a gym, and a library. The Dean family was traveling third class, so they were not traveling in luxury. Their small room was on the bottom level of the ship.

Around midnight on the fourth night at sea, a loud noise near Bertram and Eva's room woke them up. "Let's get the children dressed," Bertram told Eva. "I think the ship hit an iceberg."

By the time the Deans got to the top deck of the ship, hundreds of passengers were already there, and the crew was lowering lifeboats into the water. "Women and children first!" the crew was shouting.

Many passengers hesitated to get into the lifeboats. "This ship won't sink," they told one another. "We're safer here, on the ship."

Bertram didn't believe his family was safe on the ship. In their small room, he had felt the impact of the iceberg. Bertram was only 25 years old, and this was his first sea voyage. But he knew the damage to the ship was serious. He helped Eva into a lifeboat.

Then he handed her their two-year-old son, Bertram Jr., and their two-month-old daughter, Elizabeth. "I'll come later," he said.

Three hours later, the *Titanic* sank, and Bertram, along with 1,516 other passengers, died. The *Titanic* had a swimming pool, a gym, and a library. But it didn't have enough lifeboats for all its passengers.

At sunrise another ship rescued the *Titanic* survivors, and three days later, they arrived in New York. Eva stayed in New York for a few days and then returned to England with her children. She didn't tell them about the *Titanic* or about their father until eight years later, when she remarried. Then she told them the whole story.

Bertram Jr. and Elizabeth grew up and lived quiet lives in England. Bertram Jr. died when he was 82, and Elizabeth lived to be a very old woman.

When Elizabeth was 94 years old, she fell and broke her hip. She wanted to move into a private nursing home, but she didn't have enough money. So she began selling her *Titanic* mementos, like the suitcase her mother used for the trip back to England. Kate Winslet and Leonardo DiCaprio, the stars of the 1997 movie *Titanic*, heard that Elizabeth was selling her mementos. "Don't sell anything," they told her. "We'll take care of you." And they did. Elizabeth moved into the nursing home and had several comfortable years there. In 2009, she died in her sleep at age 97. She was the last survivor of the *Titanic*.

3 VOCABULARY

Complete the sentences with the words below.

crew	hesitated	nursing home	rescued	~~voyage~~

1. Bertram had never traveled by ship before. This was his first sea _____voyage_____.

2. The workers on the *Titanic* were lowering boats into the water. "Women and children first!" the _____ shouted.

3. Many people didn't get into the lifeboats immediately. They _____.

4. The ship that picked up the *Titanic* survivors _____ 705 passengers.

5. After Elizabeth broke her hip, she needed help walking and getting dressed. She decided to move into a _____.

④ COMPREHENSION

◆ Remembering Details

Which sentences describe the *Titanic*? Check (✔) six answers. (The first one is done for you.)

☑ It was the world's largest ship.

☐ It carried more than 2,000 passengers.

☐ All its passengers traveled in luxury.

☐ It had a swimming pool, a gym, and a library.

☐ It hit an iceberg on the fourth night of its first voyage.

☐ It sank three hours after it hit the iceberg.

☐ It was going from England to Canada.

☐ It didn't have enough lifeboats for all its passengers.

◆ Understanding Cause and Effect

Find the best way to complete each sentence. Write the letter of your answer on the line.

1. The Dean family was going to New York _c_

2. Their small room was on the bottom level of the ship ____

3. Bertram knew the damage to the ship was serious ____

4. Eva, Bertram Jr., and Elizabeth survived ____

5. Elizabeth began selling her *Titanic* mementos ____

6. She was able to live in the nursing home ____

a. because Bertram put them in a lifeboat.

b. because they were traveling third class.

c. because Bertram hoped to open a small shop in the United States.

d. because he had felt the impact of the iceberg.

e. because the stars of the 1997 movie *Titanic* helped pay for it.

f. because she needed money to pay for a private nursing home.

◆ Understanding Time Sequence

Match the events and the dates. Copy the sentences in the correct order.

The *Titanic* sank.
The last survivor of the *Titanic* died.
~~The *Titanic* left England on its first voyage.~~
The survivors of the *Titanic* arrived in New York City.
The *Titanic* hit an iceberg.

1. April 10, 1912   *The Titanic left England on its first voyage.*_____
2. April 14, 1912   _____
3. April 15, 1912   _____
4. April 18, 1912   _____
5. May 31, 2009   _____

5 DISCUSSION/WRITING

Titanic was a very popular movie. What are some other popular movies? What types of movies are they? Who stars in them? Where do they take place? What are they about? How do they end?

Play the movie riddle game with your classmates. Follow these steps.

1. What are the names of some popular movies? With your classmates, make a list on the board.

2. Choose one of the movies on the list. (Do not tell your classmates which movie you have chosen.)

3. On your own paper, answer the questions below in complete sentences.

   - What type of movie[1] is it?
   - Who is in it?
   - Where does it take place?

   - What is it about?
   - How does it end?

   Here is what one student wrote.

   - It's a science-fiction movie.
   - Harrison Ford is in it.
   - It takes place in outer space.
   - It's about an evil emperor who wants to destroy the rebels with the Death Star. The rebels' princess is his prisoner.
   - In the end, the rebels destroy the Death Star and free the princess.

4. Read your sentences to the class. Can your classmates guess which movie you chose?

---

[1] **types of movies:** action, science-fiction, horror, romantic comedy, drama

1 PRE-READING

Look at the picture.

➤ Where is the plane?

➤ Why is it there?

➤ Where are the people standing?

➤ How do you think they feel?

➤ What will happen to them?

2 READING

In the last story, you read about the last survivor of the *Titanic*. The next story is about people who survived a different disaster. What happened to them?

Read the story to find out.

MIRACLE ON THE HUDSON

On January 15, 2009, US Airways Flight 1549 took off from LaGuardia Airport in New York City. Its destination was Charlotte, North Carolina. The weather was cold, but there were no clouds or wind. It was a perfect day for flying.

Ninety seconds after takeoff, when the plane was only 3,000 feet in the air, a disaster happened: The plane flew into a flock of geese. The pilot and copilot heard the birds hit the plane: BOOM . . . BOOM . . . BOOM. Suddenly the loud noise of the engines stopped, and they made a different sound: Psssss . . . shw. Then they were silent.

Captain Chesley Sullenberger was the pilot of the plane. He was 58 years old, and he had learned to fly when he was only 16. So he had 42 years of experience. He knew the situation was very serious: He was flying a plane with no engines over a city with millions of people. But his years of experience helped him stay calm. "I can land this airplane safely," he thought. "But *where* can I land it?" He radioed air traffic control at LaGuardia.

"Hit birds," he said. "Lost both engines. Returning to LaGuardia."

"Do you want to try to land on runway 1-3?" the air traffic controller asked.

Captain Sullenberger realized there probably wasn't time to return to LaGuardia. "We're unable," he told the air traffic controller. "What's over to our right? Anything In New Jersey, maybe Teterboro Airport?"

Teterboro is a small airport in New Jersey. It is not far from New York City.

"Yes, you can land on runway 1 at Teterboro," the air traffic controller said.

Captain Sullenberger decided there wasn't time to go there, either. "We can't do it," he said.

"OK, which runway would you like?"

"We're gonna be in the Hudson."

The air traffic controller couldn't believe what he had heard. "I'm sorry, say again," he said. But he heard nothing more from Flight 1549. Twenty-two seconds later, Captain Sullenberger landed the plane on the Hudson River.

After the safe landing, the 150 passengers, the three flight attendants, and the copilot left the airplane. Some people exited through the front doors and into two inflatable life rafts. Others exited through the emergency exits and onto the wings of the airplane. Captain Sullenberger walked through the plane, which was filling with water, twice. When he was sure everybody was out, he left, too. Minutes later, boats rescued all 155 people.

People called the landing on the river the "Miracle on the Hudson," and Captain Sullenberger became a national hero. But he didn't feel like a hero. He had trouble eating and sleeping because he couldn't stop thinking about Flight 1549. But as time went by, he felt better. Nine months later, he was ready to fly again.

On October 1, 2009, Captain Sullenberger was back in the pilot's seat of a plane at LaGuardia Airport. Before the plane took off, he said over the intercom, "Ladies and gentlemen, this is Captain Sullenberger." Through the door of the cockpit, he could hear the passengers' loud applause. When they were finally quiet, he continued in his calm voice, "We'll have nice weather and smooth flying all the way to Charlotte. Welcome aboard Flight 1549."

3 VOCABULARY

Circle the word that correctly completes the sentence.

1. You are at your *destination* at the beginning / (end) of a trip.

2. When a *disaster* happens, people are happy / unhappy.

3. "*What would you like?*" is a polite way to say, "What do you want / like?"

4. You put air / water into something that is *inflatable*.

5. If you are *unable* to do something, you can / can't do it.

6. A flight is usually *smooth* if the weather is good / bad.

4 COMPREHENSION

◆ Understanding Details

Read the summary of the story "Miracle on the Hudson." There are 12 mistakes in the summary. Find the mistakes and cross them out. Write the correct words. (The first one is done for you.)

> January
On ~~June~~ 15, 2009, US Airways Flight 1522 took off from LaGuardia Airport in Los Angeles. Ninety minutes after takeoff, the plane hit a flock of ducks, and the engines went silent.

The copilot of the plane was Captain Chelsey Sullenberger, who had 14 years of experience. He realized there wasn't enough fuel to return to LaGuardia Airport or to fly to Teterboro Airport in New Mexico. He landed the plane on the Mississippi River.

The 15 passengers, the three flight attendants, the copilot, and Captain Sullenberger left the airplane. Captain Sullenberger was the first one to leave. Helicopters rescued all the survivors.

◆ Understanding Dialog

Below is the conversation between Captain Sullenberger and the air traffic controller. Some words are missing from their conversation. Write the missing words on the lines. Then practice the conversation with a partner. One student is speaker A, and the other student is speaker B.

A: Hit _____ birds _____. Lost both _____. Returning to LaGuardia.

B: Do you want to try to _____ on runway 1-3?

A: We're unable. What's over to our _____? Anything in New Jersey, maybe Teterboro _____?

B: Yes, you can land on _____ 1 at Teterboro.

A: We can't do it.

B: OK, which runway would you _____?

A: We're gonna be in the _____.

B: I'm sorry, say again.

◆ **Understanding Word Groups**

Read each group of words. One word in each group doesn't belong. Find the word and cross it out.

copilot	engines	angry	birds	disaster	airplane
flight attendants	wings	cold	cows	emergency	air traffic controller
~~driver~~	cockpit	cloudy	flock	holiday	runway
passengers	chairs	windy	geese	rescue	ship

5 DISCUSSION/WRITING

Captain Sullenberger is a national hero in the United States. Who is a national hero in your native country?

On the lines below, write a paragraph about a national hero in your native country. Be sure to write:

- the hero's name
- why he or she is a hero
- some additional information about the hero

Here is what one student wrote.

Juan Santamaría is a national hero in Costa Rica. He is a hero because he set fire to a hacienda during a battle, and he helped the Costa Rican people win a war. April 11, the day he died, is a national holiday, and our international airport is named after him.

_____

_____

_____

_____

TO THE TEACHER

The original sources of the stories in this book contain information that could not be included in the adaptations. Sometimes the information was too complicated to include; sometimes including it would have made the stories too long for the allotted space. On the other hand, the information—in many cases, the story behind the *story*—was just too interesting to leave out entirely. So, it was decided that additional facts would be given here, in a special "To the Teacher" section. Here you will also find background information on each song.

As you will see from the sophistication of the language, this section is not meant for students. You might want to offer the information only if students seem puzzled or curious, or if, in the context of the class discussion, the information would be particularly meaningful.

Also included here are supplemental listening, reading, and vocabulary activities that can be used with almost any unit, as well as specific teaching tips for the discussion/writing exercises.

 LISTENING TO THE SONG

A. Create a cloze exercise.

To generate interest in the song before listening, create a fill-in-the-blank exercise with the lyrics. Ask students to guess the missing words based on the context, reassuring them that any logical guess is correct. Students write their words in the blanks and then listen to the song to see if they guessed correctly.

B. Put the strips in order.

Copy the song and cut it into strips. (Each strip can contain one line or several lines.) In groups, students put the strips in the correct order as they listen to the song. Or distribute the strips to individual students. They come to the front of the class when they hear their lines and stand in the correct order.

 **BEFORE READING**

A. Illustrate the story.

If your students need extra support, you might want to tell them the story before they read it, stopping short of the ending. As you tell the story, draw pictures on the board to illustrate it. (An example of a basic yet clear sketch—not unlike one you might draw—is on page 19.) Following are some tips for drawing.

1. Keep it simple! To draw a person, most of the time just drawing the head and shoulders suffices—no need to draw arms, legs, feet, ears. Add a few squiggles to represent hair if the person is female. Smaller heads and shoulders are children. Add two dots for the eyes, a dot for the nose, and a line for the mouth, and the figure is complete. For example, the figures might look something like these:

2. Use the same symbols consistently to represent the same things so that students get used to your drawing style. For example, two parallel lines with a triangle-shaped roof (resembling a child's drawing of a house) represent a building. A dollar sign inside means the building is a bank; a shopping cart indicates it is a supermarket.

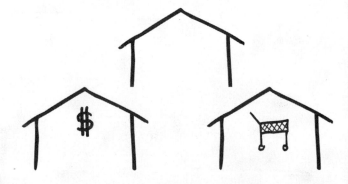

3. Draw nouns to represent verbs. For example, draw a knife to represent "to cut."

4. Feel free to move back and forth between drawing images from the story and acting out scenes. You could even pretend to take hold of items you drew on the board (such as a cup of coffee) and use them as props in your reenactment of a scene. Or you could interact with objects you drew. For example, you could knock on a picture of a door.

Drawing tips 1–3 are the suggestions of Norma Shapiro, whose reference book *Chalk Talks* (Command Performance Language Institute, 1994) has further tips and hundreds of examples of simple drawings.

B. Invent a story.

Instead of telling students the actual story, you can guide them into fabricating an alternate version of it by asking questions and encouraging students to guess the answers. Here, for example, is how a pre-reading question-and-answer session for "A Cup of Coffee and a Kidney to Go" (Story 6) might play out:

Teacher (pointing to photo):	What are the women's names?
Student:	Their names are Sarah and Katherine.
Teacher:	OK, their names are Sarah and Katherine. Where are they?
Student:	They're at a hospital.
Teacher:	OK, they're at a hospital. How do they feel?
Student:	They're happy.
Teacher:	OK, they're happy. Why are they happy?
Student:	One of the women is a grandmother for the first time.
Teacher:	OK, one of the women is a grandmother for the first time. Who is the other woman, then?
Student:	She's her sister.
Teacher:	OK, she's her sister. What are they going to do?

Student:	They're going home to tell their family about the baby.
Teacher:	(*At this point, the teacher recounts the fabricated story.*) OK, that's *our* story. Now let's read the *true* story.

Students can answer the questions orally, with volunteers guessing answers, or they can write their answers and then read them to a partner. If you choose to make this activity a whole-class effort, you can illustrate the students' answers with simple drawings on the board. (Please see the drawing tips on page 82.) After reading, you can go back to the illustrations of the fabricated story and contrast the guessed answers with the actual facts. ("We said their names were Sarah and Katherine, but they . . .")

On the website of the Minnesota Literacy Council, there is a variation of this activity called "Key Word Prediction." Choose about a dozen key words from the story. Write two of the words on the board, and ask students to make predictions about the story based on the photo and those two words. Add a few more words, and ask students to refine their predictions. Continue adding words a few at a time and asking students to alter their predictions until all of the key words are on the board.

C. Discuss first.

If you think students might have had experiences similar to those in the story, you could have them complete the discussion exercise before, rather than after, they read. For example, before reading "The King in the Nursing Home" (Story 12), you could ask students who are living in a new country how their current and past lives differ.

D. Describe the photo.

Prompt students to describe the photo by saying, "Look at the picture. What do you see?" Sometimes students respond more readily to the general question "What do you see?" than to a more specific question, such as "Who do you think these people are?" When asked a specific question, some students are reluctant to speak; they assume there is a specific correct answer. When asked, "What do you see?" they are more inclined to respond because it is clearer that any reasonable answer is acceptable.

E. Pose pre-reading questions.

If your students are comfortable speaking English, you may wish to guide them into posing their own pre-reading questions. After the class describes the photo and reads the title of the story, ask, "What do you want to know?" Write the students' questions on the board. Return to the questions after reading the story to see which were answered.

F. Ask illogical pre-reading questions.

For example, before reading "The Professor and the Peace Train" (Story 9), ask students, "Are the women from China? Are they making pots? Are they sad? Are they rich?" When the students respond "No," they will naturally supply answers that are more logical. The questions can also be phrased as statements, for example, "The women in the photo are from China, right?"

 DURING READING

A. Read aloud.

If your students understand spoken English well but have little experience reading, you may wish to begin by reading the story aloud or playing the recording of the story, perhaps stopping short of the last few paragraphs if the story has a surprise ending.

B. Predict the text.

If you are reading the story aloud to students, pause occasionally and ask them, "What will happen next?"

C. Read twice.

Students who have a tendency to stop at every unknown word should be encouraged to read the story twice, once without stopping to get the gist of the story, and then a second time, stopping to underline new vocabulary.

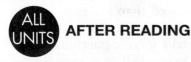 **AFTER READING**

A. Read with mistakes.

Read the story (or a section of the story) aloud, making mistakes as you read. For example, you could begin the story "A Husband and Father to Lean On" (Story 5) this way: "Bill Withers grew

up in the big city of Slab Fork, North Virginia." Students call out the errors.

B. Whisper read.

Read the story aloud. Students read along with you, mouthing the words inaudibly and trying to keep up with your pace.

C. Fill in the blanks.

This is an oral cloze activity. Read the story aloud as students follow along in their textbooks. Stop periodically and look up expectantly. Students provide the word that comes next.

D. Stand up when you hear your word.

Write key words from the story on index cards, and pass the cards out to selected students. Read the story aloud. Students stand up when they hear the words on their cards. (Because students are continually standing up and sitting down, this is sometimes called a "popcorn" activity. It is especially suitable for young learners.)

E. Rewrite the story.

If students have solid writing skills, they can rewrite the story from a different point of view. For example, Haji Ali, the chief of Korphe, could tell the story "Three Cups of Tea" (Story 10).

F. Role-play.

Students write a short skit based on the story and then act out their roles in front of the class. For example, students could role-play the conversation between Anna and Boris when they meet in Borovlyanka (Story 2).

G. Write a walking dictation.

Many units in the *True Stories* series have an "Understanding Details" exercise in which students find the incorrect word in each sentence, cross it out, and write the correct word. These sentences can be the basis of a "walking dictation." Students place their books on the opposite side of the room. They memorize the first sentence, "carry" it back to their desks, and write it down. They continue walking back and forth until they have copied all the sentences. Then they take their seats, find the incorrect word in each sentence, cross it out, and write the correct word.

H. Write a disappearing summary.

Students, working as a class, summarize the story. (Stipulate that the summary should consist of four or five sentences.) Write their summary on the board, correcting errors as you write or after the summary is complete. Read the first sentence of the summary; students repeat in unison. Erase a word or two of the sentence, and say it again; students repeat in unison. Continue erasing words a few at a time. After each erasure, say the sentence and ask students to repeat. Ultimately, students will be saying a sentence that has been totally erased. Repeat the process with the remaining sentences. When all the sentences have been erased, ask students to recite the summary from memory.

I. Write comprehension questions.

On the website of the Colorado Department of Education, Jane C. Miller suggests an activity called "In the News." Students work as a group to write comprehension questions using the WH-question words. Write their questions on the board. In pairs, students ask and answer the questions orally.

J. Check the facts.

In some units, there is an "Understanding Details" exercise in which students correct mistakes in a summary. You can easily convert this exercise into an interactive partner activity. One student reads the summary, with its mistakes, aloud. The other student turns to the story and scans to catch the mistakes—in effect, doing an instantaneous fact check. When the student scanning the story catches a mistake, he/she announces it to the partner, who corrects it in the exercise.

K. Point out cognates.

If everyone in the class has the same native language, and you have some knowledge of that language, direct students' attention to the cognates in the story. For example, below are some of the words you could highlight after reading the story "The Angel on the Subway" (Story 1) if the entire class is Hispanic. Begin by writing the list of English words on the board. Ask students to provide the Spanish counterparts to those words and write them on the board. Students pronounce the Spanish words; then you pronounce the English words. Point out the ways in which pronunciation and spelling differ. Then ask students to repeat the English words after you.

angel	ángel
university	universidad
guitar	guitarra

talent	talento
famous	famoso
train	tren
poem	poema
complete	completo

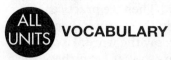

VOCABULARY

Research indicates that students' retention of new vocabulary depends not so much on the type of vocabulary exercises they complete but on how much exposure they have to the new words. The more times they "touch" a word, the more likely it is they will remember it. So you will probably want to follow up the exercises in the text with supplemental activities, such as writing the words on flash cards and presenting them again in subsequent classes. Similarly, research shows that the particular method students use to learn vocabulary—whether they write the new words on small flash cards, for example, or in a vocabulary notebook—is not as important as simply having a system for memorizing vocabulary. To promote the use of such systems, present several strategies for learning new words and encourage students to share their own techniques. Knowledge of vocabulary is a key component of reading comprehension, so it is important to devise a system for learning new words in class and to encourage students to devise their own systems for learning words at home. If your students are employed adults who have little time to study outside of class, it is particularly important to devote some class time to vocabulary study, either before or after reading.

A. Roxie Daggett, ESL specialist at Santa Fe (NM) Community College, shares this innovative pre-reading activity:

Before we read the story, we practice vocabulary I anticipate will be tricky to understand or pronounce. (Or you can have the students select the vocabulary after a first reading.) First, I write the vocabulary on the board and draw pictures or write simple definitions that the class and I come up with together. For example, for the word *exhausted* (Story 10), I might write this definition: "very tired." Then comes the fun part. We stand in a circle and create gestures that go with each word. We read the word and definition aloud together. Then I ask for a gesture, and they come up with one. (For the word *exhausted,* students might wipe their brows with the backs of their hands.) Then we practice: I say the word, and they do the gesture; then I do the gesture, and they say the word. Finally, they practice with partners so that I can check their understanding individually as one student says words and the other gestures. I learned much of this from a colleague who believes in engaging the whole body, including the sense of humor, in language acquisition.

B.   The following is another effective, no-prep activity, this one for reviewing vocabulary after reading:

1.   Select 8–10 words from the story and, at the end of class or in a subsequent class, write them on the board in random order, perhaps scattering the words across the board.

2.   Choose a word and orally describe a situation in which it could be used, but do not say the word. For example, if the target word is *lend* (Story 9), you might say, "Banks didn't _____ money to the poor people in Jobra." (Replace the word with a spoken "beep.") The context can be from the story or it can be a new context, for example: "I don't have any money with me, and I want to buy a soda. Can you _____ me a dollar?" After students call out the target word, draw a line through it. Continue giving examples and drawing lines through the remaining words.

3.   When students become comfortable with the activity, student volunteers can take turns giving examples of the target words in context. (You will need to remind them not to say the target words.) Initially they might balk, but with time they will become skilled at giving examples, sometimes from their own lives.

A game called "Flyswatter Vocabulary," appropriate for young learners, is a variation of this activity. Increase the number of vocabulary items on the board to 12–15. Students line up in two teams facing the board, about six feet from it. The students at the front of each line have flyswatters. Orally describe a situation in which one of the

words on the board could be used, but do not say the word. The first person to swat the target word with the flyswatter wins a point for his/her team. After each word, the two students with the flyswatters hand the flyswatters to the person behind them and go to the end of the line.

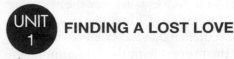

FINDING A LOST LOVE

ABOUT THE SONG

Recommended recording artist: James Blunt

"You're Beautiful" is one of the songs on James Blunt's first album. It was a number one hit in the United Kingdom, the United States, and Canada, and the only recent recording by a British singer to be a top forty hit on Latino radio stations.

ABOUT STORY 1: The Angel on the Subway

Most people believe the song "You're Beautiful" is about seeing a stranger on a subway. In fact, it was inspired by a chance encounter with an ex-girlfriend. Singer and songwriter James Blunt described his experience in an interview with the *Daily Telegraph:*

> It was a moment that I will envision forever. I saw the girl who I'd gone out with for a number of years with her new boyfriend, who I didn't know existed. It was the first time I had seen her with another man, and it gives you a bit of a jolt. She and I caught eyes and relived a lifetime, I think, in that millisecond. I thought of what could have been if the circumstances had been different. But I didn't speak, and I haven't seen her since. It's about the moment when you realize it's all just a dream.

James Blunt has not revealed the identity of the "angel on the subway"; "Sarah" is a pseudonym.

TEACHING TIP

James Blunt wrote "You're Beautiful" as a poem to his ex-girlfriend, so writing a poem about a person is an appropriate follow-up activity to this story. There are many ways to structure such a poem; searching the Internet for "name poems" or "persona poems" should yield several suggestions. Following is one possible format.

1. With the help of the class, choose the name of a famous, still-living person—a name that is familiar to everyone in the class.
2. Write the person's first name on the board. That is the first line of the poem.
3. Ask the class to supply adjectives that describe that person and make a list on the board, off to the side.
4. Choose three adjectives from the list and write them beneath the name. These three adjectives are now the second line of the poem.
5. Ask the class to supply verbs that describe what the person does and make a list on the board, off to the side.
6. Choose three verbs from the list. Add *-ing* to the stem of those verbs and write the resulting words beneath the adjectives. These words are the third line of the poem.
7. Ask the class to say complete sentences about the person. Write their sentences on the board, off to the side. Choose one sentence for the fourth line of the poem.
8. Write the person's last name as the final line of the poem.

For example, students wrote the following poem about one of their teachers:

> Jorge
> An excellent, enthusiastic, funny teacher
> Always helping people, fighting for our rights, smiling (even when he's tired)
> He might be late, but he always gives 100%.
> Islas-Martinez

Once students get the knack of writing a name poem, they can write poems about themselves or fellow students.

ABOUT STORY 2: The Return to Borovlyanka

In an interview with the *Telegraph*, Anna described coming home from work and discovering that her mother had burned everything that reminded her of Boris:

> She told me this other man was coming to meet me and that I should go out with him, and if I was lucky, he'd marry me. I burst into tears and rushed into the yard. The world turned black for me. I wanted to die, and I got a clothesline and went into a loft intending to hang myself. My mother came in and slapped me in the face and told me not to be so stupid. She persuaded me to go out with this man, and gradually he and my mother persuaded me that this was where my future lay.

Boris became a writer, and even after he married someone else, he dedicated a book to Anna.

Anna says, "Since we found each other again, I swear we haven't had a single quarrel. We've been apart for so long, and who knows how much time is left for us. We just don't want to lose time arguing."

TEACHING TIPS

A. You can easily convert the "Understanding Details" exercise to an interactive partner activity. One student reads the summary, with its mistakes, aloud. The other student turns to the story and scans to catch the mistakes—in effect, doing an instantaneous fact check. When the student scanning the story catches a mistake, he/she announces it to the partner, who corrects it in the exercise.

B. It is advisable to model the discussion/writing exercise. On the board or a piece of paper, sketch the floor plan of your favorite room. (If you draw on the board, pick a spot that can be covered later, perhaps by a retractable screen or map.) You can use circles, rectangles, and squares to represent furniture, but label everything. Show students the floor plan and explain the layout. ("My bed was here, and there was a bookcase next to the bed.") Explain why you liked the room. Then give students time to complete part A of the exercise.

Before students complete part B, describe your favorite room to them again. This time, however, do not show them your picture. As you describe the room, students draw the floor plan on their own paper. First, tell them to draw four lines to represent the walls of the room. Then orient them in the room: Ask them to imagine they are standing in the middle of the room and looking at the wall at the top of the page. To get everyone off on the right foot, you might want to draw a sketch like the one below on the board. You might also want to write key prepositional phrases on the board.

When you finish your description, show students your original picture so that they can compare it with theirs for accuracy.

C.   Another story with the theme of finding a lost loved one (in this case, a child) is "The Baby Exchange," on page 18 of *More True Stories*.

BASEBALL

ABOUT THE SONG

Recommended recording artist: Carly Simon

"Take Me Out to the Ball Game" is one of the three most frequently sung songs in the United States. (The other two are "Happy Birthday" and the national anthem.) Almost everyone who grows up in the United States knows the words to the song, although it is safe to say that very few people know the verses about Katie Casey, the "baseball mad" young woman. Newcomers to the United States who have read the lyrics to "Take Me Out to the Ball Game" in *More True Stories Behind the Songs* can justifiably feel a little smug when they hear the song sung at a baseball game: They might well be the only people in the ballpark who know that the fans are singing only the chorus of the song.

Jack Norworth got off the subway train with the complete lyrics to "Take Me Out to the Ball Game," but without the music. He took the song to composer Albert von Tilzer, who wrote the melody, a waltz in 3/4 time. In *Baseball's Greatest Hit: The Story of Take Me Out to the Ball Game*, authors Andy Strasberg, Bob Thompson, and Tim Wiles cast doubt on Norworth's own account of composing the song on a New York subway train. ("I was on the New York subway one day," Norworth said in a 1958 interview. "I took an old scrap of paper from my pocket and started writing. Fifteen minutes later, I had it.") The authors of the book support their suspicions with evidence too complicated to summarize here, but they do concede that Norworth and Tilzer probably wrote one of the best-known American songs very quickly—probably in less than an hour.

ABOUT STORY 3: Baseball Fever

The first written reference to the seventh-inning stretch is in a letter written in 1869, so the custom of standing halfway through the seventh inning is almost as old as baseball itself. Most people assume that the tradition of singing "Take Me Out to the Ball Game" goes way back, too; however, it is relatively new. As stated in the story, it began in 1976, but it didn't really catch on until 1981, when announcer Harry Caray moved from White Sox Stadium to Chicago's Wrigley Field, home of the Cubs. Cubs games were broadcast coast to coast on a cable TV network, and it was that national exposure that fostered the rapid spread of the tradition. Fans now sing the song at every major-league baseball stadium in the United States, as well as at minor-league, college, and high-school baseball fields.

TEACHING TIPS

A.   To ease students into this rather complicated story, which spans decades, it is strongly suggested that you tell students the story (actually, the two stories: the first beginning in 1908 and the second beginning in 1976) before they read it. To further facilitate comprehension, draw pictures on the board as you describe scenes from the story. (Please consult the drawing tips starting on page 82.)

B.   As a follow-up to this story, you could ask students to compare traditions associated with baseball with those of a sport that is popular in their native countries (which in most cases will turn out to be soccer). In a multinational class, students might find it interesting to learn how soccer traditions vary from country to country. To structure the discussion, begin by writing the chart on page 89 on the board. Ask students to copy the chart on their own paper and fill it in, making sure to fill in the name of the sport at the top of the chart. Students then compare their answers with those of a classmate from a different country.

Name of sport	BASEBALL	
Food fans eat	hot dogs peanuts Cracker Jacks	
Songs fans sing	the national anthem "Take Me Out to the Ball Game"	
Traditions	the seventh-inning stretch	
Season	April–October	
Starting time	1:05 or 7:05	
Ticket price	about $25	

C.   Another topic for discussion is "a song that everybody knows." Tell the students that "Take Me Out to the Ball Game" is the third most popular song in the United States. Ask them to guess which songs are in first and second place. (They are "Happy Birthday" and the national anthem.) Have students answer the questions below on their own paper and then share their writing in a small group. Invite volunteers to sing the songs for the class.

1.   What is the name of a popular song in your native country—a song that almost everybody knows?

2.   When do people sing it?

3.   What does the song mean in English? (Summarize the song in one or two sentences.)

ABOUT STORY 4: Three Strikes—And the Pitcher's Out?

It was not unheard of for Babe Ruth to strike out; he was a power hitter who generally hit the ball out of the park or missed it entirely. Still, no one could have predicted that Jackie Mitchell would strike out both Babe Ruth and Lou Gehrig. The Lookouts

manager knew good publicity when he saw it. He decided to quit while he was ahead after Jackie struck out Gehrig and immediately pulled her out of the game.

It is hard to say with certainty what was behind the baseball commissioner's decision to bar Jackie Mitchell from professional baseball. The Yankees-Lookouts game was filmed, and he undoubtedly saw the ten-minute ovation fans gave Jackie. He may have feared the disruptive effect a female pitcher could have on the game. Or he may have been bowing to pressure from players like Babe Ruth, who was outspoken in his opposition to playing with women.

It is also hard to say what kind of career Jackie Mitchell might have had as a professional baseball player. What is certain, however, is that she had genuine talent, as evidenced by this March 31, 1931 quote from the *Chattanooga News*: "She uses an odd, side-armed delivery, and puts both speed and curve on the ball. Her greatest asset, however, is control. She can place the ball where she pleases, and her knack at guessing the weakness of a batter is uncanny." After the April 2 game, the *New York Times* predicted that "she may win laurels this season which cannot be ascribed to mere gallantry. The prospect grows gloomier for misogynists."

TEACHING TIPS

A.   To facilitate students' comprehension of the story, which has many baseball terms, consider completing the vocabulary exercise with students *before* they read. Using the drawing in the exercise as a model, create the baseball scene on the board and, together with the students, label the people and things in your drawing. (There is often at least one student with baseball experience who will be able to identify some items.)

B.   A game of classroom baseball is a nice follow-up to this unit. The batters are the students, divided into two teams, and you are the pitcher for both teams. Your "pitches" are based on vocabulary items, verb forms, or grammatical structures that you want to reinforce. For example, if your students need practice forming the past-tense forms of irregular verbs, you can "pitch" the infinitive form, and the batter has to say the past tense form correctly in order to advance to first base. Batters who answer incorrectly are "out." (A batter is out after only one strike, not three.) You can draw a baseball diamond on the board to record players' progress, or the classroom can become a baseball diamond if you designate the four corners of the room as bases; players move around the room as they advance from base to base. After three outs, a side is retired, and the other side gets a chance. Before you begin playing, announce how many innings you will play. If time allows, you can go into extra innings in case of a tie.

C. Students who particularly enjoyed the stories in this unit would also enjoy the story "Love or Baseball?" on page 38 of *True Stories in the News*. The story is about a young man whose baseball fever got him into a real predicament with his girlfriend. (That story is at the beginning, not high-beginning, level, so students should find it a bit easier to read.)

 UNIT 3

SOMEBODY TO LEAN ON

ABOUT THE SONG

Recommended recording artist: Bill Withers

(Please note: On the recommended recording, Withers begins the song, "Sometimes in my life," although the official lyrics are "Sometimes in our lives." The official lyrics fit grammatically with the rest of the verse, so those are the lyrics reprinted here.)

The song "Lean on Me" is from Bill Withers' second album, *Still Bill*, released in 1972. The song exhibits Withers' signature style of simple lyrics. "I'm a stickler for saying something the simplest possible way with some elements of poetry," he said in an interview for the website Songfacts. "Simple is memorable." He characterized "Lean on Me" as "a rural song that translates across demographic lines. Who could argue with the fact that it would be nice to have somebody who really was that way? My experience was, there were people who were that way. They would help you out."

ABOUT STORY 5: A Husband and Father to Lean On

After Bill Withers' father died, his mother and grandmother raised him in Slab Fork and in the nearby town of Beckley. (His song "Grandma's Hands" is a tribute to his grandmother.) Slab Fork was a true mining town: The mining company owned not only the mine but also the houses where the miners' families lived and the grocery store where they shopped. The current population of Slab Fork is 200.

Bill Withers had no formal training as a musician. According to his official website, he began writing songs in the navy simply to express what he felt. He wrote three hit songs—all Grammy winners—in relatively short succession: "Ain't No Sunshine," "Lean on Me," and "Just the Two of Us." Then he abruptly disappeared from the music scene. (The photo of Bill Withers that accompanies this story is from 1985, the year he quit the music business.) He was out of the public eye until 2009, when he participated in a documentary about him, titled *Still Bill*. On the website realpoliticalfacetalk, the filmmaker, Alex Flack, explained why he thought Mr. Withers had stayed out of the music spotlight for so long: "The answer is simple but subtle and does take a whole film to discuss. But in short, music, and more particularly the music business—touring, etc.—just did not define him. It was important for him to be around for his family rather than out there, hustling all the time."

TEACHING TIPS

A. In the comprehension exercise "Understanding the Main Ideas," students complete the answers to the questions. A question-and-answer exercise can subsequently become a small-group activity if, after completing the exercise in writing, students ask one another the questions. Teacher Lisa McKinney recommends structuring the activity this way:

1. The teacher asks the first question and calls on a student to read the answer.

2. After reading the answer, that student poses the second question to another student.

3. That student answers the second question and poses the third question to another student, and so on.

Ms. McKinney cautions her students to call on one another by name—no pointing or saying, "You, next." She calls this activity "Pass the Question" and remarks, "There are often grimaces, groans, and lots of grins as students force one another to participate."

B.   Laurel Pollard and Natalie Hess describe the activity in the discussion/writing exercise in their teacher resource book *Zero Prep* (Alta Book Center Publishers, page 16, "Things I Need," 1997). The authors advise that in large classes it might be best to have students write their lists on their own paper and then post the papers around the room. Students circulate, read the lists, and write their names next to things they think they can help with. In smaller classes, it can be a whole-group activity: Students read their lists aloud, and classmates who think they can help raise their hands. Students then mingle to get information from their classmates. Students could revisit their list a few weeks later and, as a follow-up activity, write how and where they found the things they needed.

ABOUT STORY 6: A Cup of Coffee and a Kidney to Go

Annamarie Ausnes had a genetic condition known as polycystic kidney disease, and her kidney function was only 15 percent. Her doctors told her that when the function dropped below 12 percent, she would have to begin dialysis while she waited for a transplant. A wait of several years would be almost inevitable. In an interview with the *New York Times*, Annamarie related that the transplant coordinator at the hospital had told her, "You never know where a donor's going to come from. Keep telling your story." So when Annamarie told Sandra about her medical condition, it wasn't a totally spontaneous revelation.

Sandra Andersen, who did volunteer work in Mexico and dug mud out of houses in New Orleans after Hurricane Katrina, believed her gesture was not unusually magnanimous. "People should give freely of themselves," she said, "and they do more often than is noticed."

TEACHING TIPS

A.   In the discussion/writing exercise, students make a list of good topics for small talk. On the website About.com, teacher and teacher trainer Kenneth Beare gives a list of common small-talk subjects in an article titled "Appropriate Subjects for Small Talk." If your students have trouble coming up with topics, you might suggest these: sports, hobbies, weather, family (general questions, not questions about private matters), media (films, books, magazines, and websites), holidays, hometown, job (general questions, not too specific), latest fashions and trends, and celebrity gossip. He also gives a list of topics that aren't very good for small talk: salary, politics, intimate relationships, religion, death, personal finances, and sales (trying to sell something to someone you have just met). Making small talk can actually be a little tricky because topics that are appropriate in one culture may be inappropriate in another. If time allows, help students generate a second list— topics to avoid when making small talk with native speakers of English.

B. There are several stories in *More True Stories* with a "Somebody to Lean On" theme. Any one of them would be a fitting companion to the song and stories in this unit. They are "Pay It Forward" (page 34), "The Auction" (page 54), and "Two Strangers" (page 86).

UNIT 4   A SIMPLE LIFE

ABOUT THE SONG

Recommended recording artists: Yo-Yo Ma and Alison Krauss

Historically, the words *turn, turn* have had a literal as well as a figurative meaning; they indicated the dancers were to turn. How do we know that? Musicologist Roger Hall, who is an expert in Shaker music, states that Shaker hymns usually have two or more stanzas, whereas Shaker songs have only one stanza. "Simple Gifts," with its one verse, was clearly a dance song, complete with instructions to the dancers.

The opening line is "'Tis *the* gift to be simple" and not "'Tis *a* gift to be simple," as it is often sung. Various singers and arrangers over the years changed the word. "To the Shakers," Dr. Hall writes, "that one word makes a big difference! They are talking about *the gift* from God, not just any gift."

ABOUT STORY 7: The Last Three?

Students may wonder how three people—a middle-aged man and two elderly women—could possibly maintain a farm. Dozens of volunteers come to the farm twice a year to work. They paint fences, fix screen doors, clean windows, stack firewood, and generally do what needs to be done. The admission fees paid by the 10,000 tourists who visit the farm every year also support it.

What will happen to the farm (called Sabbathday Lake) if the three people in the story turn out to be the last three Shakers on earth? The future of the farm is entrusted to two nonprofit foundations that will protect the land from being developed or subdivided. Most likely it will become a museum, as have other defunct Shaker communities.

On the website of one such community, Canterbury Shaker Village, there is a succinct history of the Shaker religion:

> The religious group that we know today as the Shakers was formed in 18th-century England when dissidents from various religions, including English Quakers and Methodists, formed a religious society based on prophetic doctrine. The group, formally called the United Society of Believers, was known as Shaking Quakers, or Shakers, because of their use of ecstatic dance in worship. The Shakers emigrated to the United States in 1774 and eventually established 19 self-contained communities from Maine to Kentucky. . . . The Shakers' revolutionary Christianity shocked their contemporaries. They challenged almost every mainstream ideal of American society during their time. Shakers believed in community ownership, pacifism, dancing in worship, equality of the sexes, celibacy, and living simply.

The Shakers are sometimes confused with the Amish because both groups strive to live simply; however, there are some significant differences. Amish families are generally large; Shakers are celibate. The Amish live apart from modern society, whereas the Shakers interact with the outside world. (The Shakers have phones, television, and Internet access.) The Amish live in close-knit communities, but the Shakers go one step further and live communally.

Both the Amish and the Shakers emphasize the importance of the group over the individual. In the late 1800s, the Shakers at Sabbathday Lake removed the markers from every grave in their cemetery and replaced them with a single slab of granite over the entrance. The sign bears one word: SHAKERS.

TEACHING TIP

In the unit opener, students draw while they listen to the song. Before class, listen to the song yourself and make your own drawing (perhaps the more free-form, the better) and offer that as a model so that students have a clear idea of the task.

ABOUT STORY 8: A Wonderful Gift?

As a child, Dorian Paskowitz was severely asthmatic. One day he saw a newspaper photo of three men surfing in Southern California. "If I lived there," he told his mother, "I wouldn't be sick anymore." The Paskowitz family lived near an oil refinery in Texas, and his mother suspected that Dorian might be right—that his asthma would improve if he were breathing unpolluted air. She and her husband talked it over, and they decided to move to California. Dorian became an expert surfer, and his health was restored. Even after he became a doctor (his medical degree is from Stanford University), he remained convinced that surfing was the best medicine. He practiced medicine full-time for a few years but abandoned his practice to travel the world as a surfer. Now in his late 80s, Dorian Paskowitz still surfs every day.

Some of the Paskowitz children now resent being denied a formal education. In a 2008 interview with *Surfing* magazine, Dorian gave this rationale for keeping his children out of school:

> I *never* intended to send the kids to school. Ever. I wanted them to surf. They can go to school now; they're 50 years old. But they can't do the things they did when they were surfing. When they were the last ones out at big Pipeline or when my son Israel won the championship in Australia. They can't do that now.

In 1972, the Paskowitz family opened a surf camp in San Diego, California. It is still in operation and offers a day camp for autistic children. The day camp is overseen by Israel Paskowitz, whose son Isaiah is autistic. Israel discovered that Isaiah seemed to benefit from surfing with him—that the ocean had the same therapeutic effect on his son's autism that it had had on his father's asthma—and he wanted other autistic children to experience that benefit. The day camp, Surfers Healing, is free and is staffed by volunteers.

Dorian is credited with introducing surfing to the country of Israel in 1956, and he is passionate about effecting a positive change in Israeli-Arab relations through surfing. In 2007, at age 86, he and his oldest son, David, traveled to Gaza to donate surfboards to young men there. A newspaper photo that Dorian had seen of two Palestinian surfers sharing one surfboard prompted the trip. In a 2010 interview with the *San Francisco Sentinel*, Dorian told a reporter, "They just looked so forlorn. So my son David and I said, 'Well, let's go take 'em some boards.'" While in the Middle East, Dorian co-founded a charity called Surfing 4 Peace.

UNIT 5 THE WAY TO PEACE

ABOUT THE SONG

Recommended recording artist: Cat Stevens

The singer and composer Cat Stevens recorded "Peace Train" in 1971. Like John Lennon's "Give Peace a Chance," it has been an anthem of numerous peace movements over the decades.

Cat Stevens changed his name to Yusuf Islam in the late 1970s but now goes by simply "Yusuf." At the height of his success (he had sold 23 million recordings, including the hits "Wild World," "Morning Has Broken," "Moon Shadow," and "Peace Train"), Cat Stevens almost drowned while swimming at Malibu Beach in California. After his near-death experience, he converted to Islam, changed his name, abandoned the music business, and moved back to London, his birthplace. After a 28-year hiatus, he has recently resumed composing and recording songs.

As of this writing, Yusuf's performance of "Peace Train" at the Nobel Concert can be viewed on YouTube under the title "Yusuf (Cat Stevens) Peace Train-Nobel Concert 2006."

ABOUT STORY 9: The Professor and the Peace Train

Initially, Professor Yunus worked through already existing banks to lend money to the poor by guaranteeing the loans himself. Over the course of several years, his loan program expanded from one village to one hundred villages in Bangladesh. At that point, Professor Yunus became convinced that he had a viable business model and decided to set up a bank that would make loans exclusively to the poor.

Grameen Bank lends people money to buy the materials they need to make their products or to buy the tools they need to earn a living—a pair of scissors, for example, for cutting hair. The bank also grants housing loans, most of them for about $300. That amount allows people in developing countries to build a house with a tin roof, concrete columns, and a sanitary latrine.

Borrowers are required to pay back the entire amount they borrow with interest within one year. Ninety-eight percent of borrowers do so. The high repayment rate is probably due in part to Grameen's procedure for granting loans. People must apply in groups of five. Each person in the group vouches for the other four, so group members go over one another's business plans before they put together their loan application and encourage one another in their enterprises.

The World Bank reported that one-third of the people who borrow from the Grameen Bank cross over the poverty line. Muhammad Yunus's goal is nothing short of creating a poverty-free world. "My fondest dream," he says, "is that someday our next generations, our children and grandchildren, will go to the museums to see what poverty was like because there will no longer be any on this planet. I believe that day will come."

The 2006 Nobel Peace Prize was $1.4 million, to be divided equally between Muhammad Yunus and the Grameen Bank. Professor Yunus announced that he would use his share of the money to create a company that will make inexpensive, nutritious food for the poor and to establish an eye hospital for the poor in Bangladesh.

ABOUT STORY 10: Three Cups of Tea

The information in the story is from the young reader's edition of *Three Cups of Tea* by Greg Mortenson and David Oliver Relin. Due to space constraints, several key parts in the account had to be omitted, most notably the fact that when Greg returned to Korphe with the funds to build the school, Haji Ali pointed out that there was no way to get the building materials over the ravine that separated Korphe from the rest of the world. Before they could build the school, they had to build a bridge. Greg returned to the United States and asked Jean Hoerni to finance the bridge, and he gave Greg an additional $10,000. When the school was finished, Greg brought Jean a picture of the school, as promised. Jean was critically ill then and hospitalized. Greg hung a picture of the Korphe school in Jean's hospital room. A nurse by profession, Greg took care of Jean during the last weeks of his life.

After the school was built, Haji Ali revealed to Greg that he was illiterate. Holding his Koran, he said, "I can't read it. I can't read anything. This is the greatest sadness in my life. I'll do anything so the children of my village never have to know this feeling."

More information about Greg Mortenson's endeavors is on the website of the Central Asia Institute.

TEACHING TIPS

A. In the discussion/writing exercise, students write about hospitality customs in their native countries. You could prompt students with some of the following questions:

- Are there any special words you say to greet your guests?
- Do you greet your guests by kissing them (how many times?), shaking their hands, bowing, or putting your hand on your heart?
- Is there a special food or drink you offer guests?
- How many times do you offer your guests something to eat or drink?

- Do you give your guests slippers to wear?
- Do you try to look busy (so your guests know that everything is taken care of), or do you try to look relaxed?
- If guests bring you a gift, do you open it immediately or later?
- If your guests come by car, do you walk them to their car at the end of their visit, or do you say goodbye at the door?
- What do you do when strangers (for example, someone selling something) come to your door?
- If you come to someone's home as a guest, do you bring a gift?
- If so, what is a good gift to bring?
- Are there any things you never give as gifts?
- Do you wrap the gift in special paper? (What colors should the paper be?)
- Do you offer the gift with one hand or two hands?
- Do you bring flowers? (What kind? What color? How many?)
- When you arrive, do you take off your coat and hat outside the home or inside the home?
- Do you arrive on time or late? (How late?)
- Is it polite to take second or third helpings of food?
- Do you leave a little food on your plate, or do you eat everything on your plate?

B. Greg Mortenson says that Haji Ali was the wisest person he ever knew. For additional writing and speaking practice, students could complete these sentences: "The wisest person I ever knew was _____. He/She was wise because _____." They could then share their writing with the class, giving concrete examples of what the wise person said or did that demonstrated wisdom.

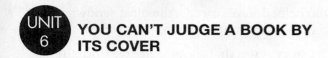

UNIT 6 — YOU CAN'T JUDGE A BOOK BY ITS COVER

ABOUT THE SONG

Recommended recording artist: Susan Boyle

The musical *Les Miserables*, written in 1980 by a French composer and a French lyricist, was only moderately successful in France. Five years later, the English-language version debuted in London. That production was wildly successful, as was its 1987 debut on Broadway. (The Broadway production won eight Tony awards.) It became one of the most popular musicals of all time: 38 countries have hosted performances in 21 languages. Susan Boyle's performance of "I Dreamed a Dream" sparked renewed interest in a musical that was already beloved by many.

ABOUT STORY 11: Susan's Got Talent

Susan's mother was her best friend and staunchest supporter. When she died at age 91, Susan was so grief-stricken that she didn't sing for two years. When her grief began to lessen, Susan began to think again about pursuing a career as a professional singer—a dream her mother had steadfastly encouraged. She decided to enter the contest as a tribute to her mother.

Susan's international debut in the talent show was only the first round of the contest. She won the next round (she sang the song "Memories" from the musical *Cats*), but she failed to win the final contest, coming in second to a dance group. Although she did not win the top prize of 100,000 pounds, sales of her CD, released a few months later, more than compensated her for that loss. It immediately went triple platinum, with sales of over 3 million in the first few weeks after its release.

TEACHING TIPS

A. It is not necessary to explain every word and every grammatical construction in every song. But because the word *would* occurs repeatedly in this song, you might want to explain its meaning here. The word has several uses. It describes circumstances that are contrary to fact (*If I had more money, I would buy a new car.*); it softens requests (*Would you please help me?*); it describes actions done habitually in the past (*Whenever I was sick, my mother would give me chamomile tea.*); and it is the past-tense form of *will*, most commonly used in reported speech (*She said she would come.*). In the song, *would* is a past-tense form, used in this case not to report past utterances but past dreams and prayers. Students quickly grasp the meaning of the word if you have them practice transforming direct quotes in the future tense (*She said, "I will come."*) to indirect quotes (*She said she would come.*).

B. In Part A of the discussion/writing exercise, students write as many sentences as they can about their partners. You could turn this into a contest by giving a small prize to the student who writes the most sentences.

C. In Part B of the discussion/writing exercise, students discuss the meaning of the saying "You can't judge a book by its cover." You could also discuss other sayings about appearance, for example:

All that glitters is not gold.
Beauty is only skin deep.
Beauty is in the eye of the beholder.
Handsome is as handsome does.
Still waters run deep.

ABOUT STORY 12: The King in the Nursing Home

After Charles Mumbere left the United States, his supervisor at the Pennsylvania nursing home where he had worked remembered him fondly in an interview with the Harrisburg *Patriot-News*. "He was quiet, loyal, a very hard worker, and a very nice person," she said. "Nobody knew. I'm quite happy for him. He was well liked here. Everybody said he was very polite and really kind."

In an e-mail interview with the same newspaper, Charles sent his regards to his former coworkers. "Greetings to my American friends," he wrote. "I have missed my friends in the U.S.A. and the country itself." Charles said that he had felt comfortable living in the United States during his unexpected 22-year stay. "It's a very big country—it's like an ocean," he said. "In an ocean, you find very many creatures there. I felt at home because the United States has all the races in the world." Charles expects to return to the United States regularly to visit because he has a son who lives with his ex-wife in Virginia.

TEACHING TIPS

A.   The first paragraph of the reading invites speculation. You might wish to read that paragraph aloud, with students following along in their books. Stop after the first paragraph and ask students, "Why was a king working as a nurse's aide?" After students have offered some possible reasons, continue reading the story. You could, in fact, stop after every paragraph and ask students to speculate on how the story will continue.

B.   For another story with a "You Can't Judge a Book by Its Cover" theme, please see "The Husband" on page 50 of *More True Stories*.

 UNIT 7 GREAT ESCAPES

ABOUT THE SONG

Recommended recording artist: Richie Havens

"Follow the Drinking Gourd" was first published in 1928. A new version of the song, with the added line "For the old man is waiting to carry you to freedom," was published in 1947 and later recorded by the Weavers, a folk music quartet. The origin of the song has not been determined.

ABOUT STORY 13: The Drinking Gourd

In classrooms all over the United States, elementary schoolchildren learn the story of Peg-leg Joe as a true story. Teachers use the story and the song "Follow the Drinking Gourd" to introduce children to the topics of slavery and the Underground Railroad. Is the story true? Slaves were not allowed to learn to read or write, so it is likely that directions to routes north were transmitted orally. However, historians doubt that this song, as it is written now, guided slaves to freedom. Slave owners and bounty hunters would surely have discovered a route marked by symbols on dead trees. As for the figure of Peg-leg Joe, historians surmise that he is a composite of people

who helped slaves escape, the most renowned of whom was Harriet Tubman.

The story states that slaves were free once they crossed the Ohio River. That was true in theory. Until its repeal in 1864, the Fugitive Slave Act permitted the capture of escaped slaves even after they crossed the Ohio. So escaped slaves were not truly safe unless they continued north to Canada.

TEACHING TIPS

A.   In the unit opener, students are asked what the Big Dipper is called in their native languages. It is described as a dipper, or ladle, in languages other than English, but it is likely that students will also submit other descriptive names, such as the saucepan, the great wagon, the great cart, the salmon net, or the seven sages.

You will note that the Big Dipper is referred to as a "group of stars," rather than as a constellation. That designation is not only linguistically easier for students but is also scientifically correct. The Big Dipper is an asterism—a group of easily recognizable stars—in the constellation Ursa Major. To find Polaris (the North Star), follow the two outside stars in the bowl of the Big Dipper. Draw an imaginary line from the bottom star to the top star, and extend the line about five times the distance between those two stars. The North Star is at the end of that imaginary line.

B.   In the story and vocabulary exercise, a gourd is described as a vegetable. Like the tomato and the pumpkin, it is actually a fruit, but as most people call it a vegetable, it is defined as such.

ABOUT STORY 14: Twelve Kilometers to a New Life

Originally Günter Wetzel and his family planned to go with the Strelzyks on the first flight. But Günter's wife, Petra, began having nightmares about the balloon flight. Their children were small, and she was worried about their safety. In the eleventh hour, the Wetzel family backed out. Even though the balloon didn't make it over the wall on the first try, that flight convinced Petra that the plan was feasible, and ultimately the Wetzels left East Germany with the Strelzyks.

Most English-language accounts of "The Great Balloon Escape" have a happy ending: They conclude with the landing of the balloon in West Germany. In a 2002 interview, however, Peter Strelzyk revealed that a truly happy ending was some time in coming. Within hours of the balloon's landing in West Germany, East German police arrested Peter's brother, sister, and brother-in-law. Although they had known nothing of Peter's plan, they were sentenced to two years in prison. Peter's close friend and colleague Thomas Dietrich was also arrested. With the help of Amnesty International, Peter was able to obtain the release of his relatives, but he was not able to free his friend Thomas. In 1982, the East German police released Thomas from prison only after he signed agreements in which he promised to spy on Peter Strelzyk. He was given a false identity and allowed to move to West Germany, where he resumed his friendship with Peter. Thomas provided the East German police with information on Peter and his family for years.

In 1998, Peter and his wife returned to their hometown to live in the house they had abandoned in 1979. "The reasons we had for leaving had all disappeared," Peter explained. When he returned home, Peter asked to see the files that the East German police had kept on him through the years. In those files, weighing 25 kilograms, he discovered that his friend Thomas had been an informant.

TEACHING TIP

The 1982 Disney movie *Night Crossing* is based on a book by Peter's wife, Doris. As of this writing, the DVD is available at a reasonable price (about $13). Chapter 11, "To Freedom," is a dramatic reenactment of the successful balloon flight. About 14 minutes long, the chapter has only minimal dialog and is suitable for classroom viewing. (The movie shows the balloon catching fire on takeoff. That actually happened; Günter extinguished the flame.)

SURVIVORS

ABOUT THE SONG

Recommended recording artist: Celine Dion

James Horner wrote the melody of the song "My Heart Will Go On" for the movie *Titanic*. The music was intended to be a leitmotif throughout the film. As an afterthought, he asked Will Jennings to write lyrics for his music. The song would be played after the movie, while the credits rolled. The movie's director, James Cameron, initially resisted adding the song but ultimately agreed to include it. Likewise, Celine Dion resisted recording it but eventually did, a cappella and in one take. (The instrumental accompaniment was added later.) The song was an international hit and Celine Dion's best-selling single.

ABOUT STORY 15: The Littlest Passenger

Elizabeth Dean went by the name of Millvina (although Elizabeth was her actual name), and most news accounts identify her as Millvina. She is Elizabeth in this story because the name is more familiar to students.

Millvina told a BBC interviewer in 1998 that she believed her father's swift actions had saved his family. "That's partly what saved us—because he was so quick," she said. "Some people thought the ship was unsinkable." Millvina's mother told her that her father had wrapped her in a sack he had found on deck to protect her against the bitterly cold air.

In an interview with the Associated Press, Millvina Dean said she was relieved that she had no memories of the sinking of the *Titanic*. "I wouldn't want to remember it, really," she said. In 1958, she and other *Titanic* survivors went to see the movie *A Night to Remember*, about the *Titanic*. She found the movie so upsetting that she declined to see the 1997 movie *Titanic*.

Kate Winslet and Leonardo DiCaprio contributed to a fund that had already been established to help Millvina with her expenses. As a British citizen, she could have resided at a free government-run facility but preferred the private nursing home, which had more amenities.

In addition to the suitcase, other *Titanic* mementos on the auction block were her mother's letters from the Titanic Relief Fund, which offered the young widow one pound, seven shillings and sixpence (less than $2.00) a week for the rest of her life as compensation for her husband's death.

TEACHING TIPS

A.   In the unit opener, students write dictations of four verses of the song in small groups, with each group deciding on a final version to write on the board. This collaborative activity generally results in the most accurate writing when students divvy up the writing before they listen. (Student A writes the first line of the verse, Student B the second, etc.) You might want to tell students to discuss a strategy before they listen.

B.   In the pre-reading exercise, students are asked to tell what they know about the *Titanic*. This affords an opportunity to introduce students to the concept of idea mapping. As students provide information, organize it on the board in clusters of topics and subtopics. (If you are not familiar with this technique, you will find examples of idea maps and other graphic organizers on the Internet. The websites of school districts generally have the most helpful examples.)

C.   The discussion/writing exercise is from the website Lanternfish ESL. Chris Gunn, the creator of the "Movie Riddle" game, begins the activity this way:

> I tell my students, "I'm trying to remember the name of a movie, but I can't think of it. What was that movie called? Hmm."

> I wait a few seconds to see how the students respond. They might ask me a question such as, "Do you remember who is in it?" or something similar. If no one asks, then I begin a description like the one below until somebody can help me remember.

> "You know, it's a drama. Julia Roberts is in it. It takes place in a town in California where many people got sick. She plays a secretary who works for a law firm. The movie is about a company that tries to hide its chemical pollution that killed many people. In the end,

the company loses the law case and has to pay millions of dollars."

> If somebody calls out the answer, then I take out a chocolate and toss it to them. The class usually perks up at that point. Then I begin another movie riddle. I quickly give them more movie riddles so that they can experience all of the important language points before they write their own movie riddles.

ABOUT STORY 16: Miracle on the Hudson

As a young man at the United States Air Force Academy, Captain Sullenberger had trained as a glider pilot, and he still flies gliders as a hobby. Many news reports attributed his success in landing the disabled airplane in part to his experience as a glider pilot. However, in his book *Highest Duty*, Captain Sullenberger writes:

> I have to dispel that notion. The flight characteristics and speed and weight of an Airbus are completely different from the characteristics of the gliders I flew. It's a night-and-day difference. So my glider training was of little help. Instead, I think what helped me was that I had spent years flying jet airplanes and had paid close attention to energy management. On thousands of flights, I had tried to fly the optimum flight path. I think that helped me more than anything else on Flight 1549. I was going to try to use the energy of the Airbus, without either engine, to get us safely to the ground . . . or somewhere.

In an interview with Katie Couric on *60 Minutes*, Captain Sullenberger revealed that he was initially uncomfortable with his status as a national hero but later came to understand and accept it. "People want good news," he said. "They want to feel hopeful. And if I can help in that way, I will."

TEACHING TIPS

A.   As of this writing, it is possible to listen on the Internet to the exchange between the air traffic controller and Captain Sullenberger (who is addressed as "Cactus 1549"). Some sites give both audio and written transcripts. Although the voices of the men remain calm, an error that both make reveals their underlying stress: They misidentify the flight number, sometimes calling it Flight 1539 and sometimes Flight 1529. As a targeted listening activity, students might listen for the mistake. (A word of caution: Listening to the audio transcript is fascinating and at the same time unsettling. Some might find the experience intolerably stressful.)

B.   There are three stories in *More True Stories* with a "Survivors" theme. Any one of them would be a fitting companion to the stories in this unit. They are "Everybody's Baby" (page 30), "A Long Fishing Trip" (page 66), and "The Surgeon" (page 70).

ANSWER KEY

UNIT 1

Story 1: The Angel on the Subway

VOCABULARY

2. keep in touch
3. lost touch
4. fiancé
5. crowd
6. perhaps

UNDERSTANDING THE MAIN IDEAS

1. c
2. a
3. b

UNDERSTANDING TIME RELATIONSHIPS

2. e
3. d
4. a
5. c

UNDERSTANDING DETAILS

2. ~~Canada~~/Kosovo
3. ~~violin~~/guitar
4. ~~poet~~/songwriter
5. ~~big~~/small
6. ~~happy~~/famous
7. ~~Paris~~/ London
8. ~~days~~/hours

Story 2: The Return to Borovlyanka

VOCABULARY

2. a different
3. many
4. no
5. long
6. fast
7. worried
8. happy

UNDERSTANDING DETAILS

~~1956~~/1946; ~~Friday~~/Tuesday; ~~faraway~~/nearby; ~~months~~/days; ~~brother~~/father; ~~years~~/months; ~~60~~/80; ~~apartment~~/house; ~~wife's~~/parents'; ~~40~~/60; ~~hours~~/weeks

UNDERSTANDING TIME AND PLACE

WHEN: a few days later; this evening; eventually

WHERE: across the road; in a nearby village; at work; near the house

UNDERSTANDING PRONOUNS

2. h
3. b
4. d
5. g
6. e
7. a
8. f

UNIT 2

Story 3: Baseball Fever

VOCABULARY

2. f
3. a
4. b
5. c
6. d

UNDERSTANDING THE MAIN IDEAS

2. b, c
3. a, b
4. a, b
5. a, c
6. a, b

UNDERSTANDING ADJECTIVE CLAUSES

2. a
3. b
4. c
5. d

UNDERSTANDING TIME AND PLACE

WHEN: during the seventh inning, in the spring of 1908, a few days later

WHERE: in New York City, in Chicago, around the world, at baseball stadiums in Japan

Story 4: Three Strikes—And the Pitcher's Out?

VOCABULARY

b. 2
c. 4
d. 6
e. 1
f. 3
g. 5
h. 8

UNDERSTANDING THE MAIN IDEAS

2. The ball comes to the plate in a straight line and then suddenly drops.
3. Four thousand people came.
4. They wanted to see me pitch to Babe Ruth and Lou Gehrig.
5. He threw his bat down and walked angrily away from the plate.
6. He thought that baseball was "too strenuous" for a woman.
7. I returned to my hometown, got a job, and later married.

UNDERSTANDING A SUMMARY

a

FINDING INFORMATION

2. three and a half pounds
3. she was tiny
4. they made sure she got plenty of exercise
5. six
6. her father
7. in their yard

Story 5: A Husband and Father to Lean On

VOCABULARY
2. a hand
3. melody
4. quit
5. faraway

UNDERSTANDING THE MAIN IDEAS
2. were miners
3. were poor
4. leaned on one another
5. left home to join the U.S. Navy
6. wrote songs in his free time
7. was a good beginning for a song
8. is about the people in Slab Fork

UNDERSTANDING CAUSE AND EFFECT
2. c
3. d
4. e
5. a

UNDERSTANDING TIME SEQUENCE
2. He joined the U.S. Navy.
3. He moved to Los Angeles.
4. He wrote the hit song "Lean On Me."
5. He quit the music business.

Story 6: A Cup of Coffee and a Kidney to Go

VOCABULARY
2. YES
3. NO
4. YES
5. NO
6. YES

UNDERSTANDING THE MAIN IDEAS
1. b
2. a
3. c
4. c

FINDING MORE INFORMATION
2. e
3. d
4. a
5. b

UNDERSTANDING DIALOG
disease, worse, transplant donate
son
tested

UNIT
4

THE SONG
2. b
3. e
4. c
5. f
6. a
7. d
8. d

Story 7: The Last Three?

VOCABULARY
1. orchard
2. communally
3. inauguration
4. elderly

REMEMBERING DETAILS
He lives on a farm in Maine.
He gets up early every morning.
He works hard every day.
He is a Shaker.

FINDING INFORMATION
2. 19
3. one
4. in Maine
5. visit the farm
6. Arnold Hadd
7. the rules that Shakers live by
8. about ten
9. not one person
10. three

CHECKING FACTS
YES: 2, 5, 6, 10
NO: 1, 3, 7, 9
NOT IN STORY: 4, 8

Story 8: A Wonderful Gift?

VOCABULARY
2. thought it over
3. barefoot
4. allow, fast food

UNDERSTANDING THE MAIN IDEAS
2. met in 1957
3. was an opera singer
4. had nine children
5. lived in a camper
6. traveled all over the world
7. worked as a doctor
8. have mixed feelings

UNDERSTANDING CONTRASTS
2. f
3. a
4. b
5. e
6. d

UNDERSTANDING A SUMMARY
a

UNIT 5

THE SONG

The words *peace train* are in the song 23 times.

Story 9: The Professor and the Peace Train

VOCABULARY

1. profit
2. lend
3. materials
4. whenever

UNDERSTANDING THE MAIN IDEAS

2. economics
3. village
4. poor
5. pocket
6. market
7. small
8. Peace

UNDERSTANDING A SUMMARY

b

UNDERSTANDING DIALOG

bamboo	borrow
buy	end
costs	profit

Story 10: Three Cups of Tea

VOCABULARY

2. e
3. a
4. b
5. c
6. d

UNDERSTANDING DETAILS

third/second; 6/600; woman/man; her/him;
up/down; weeks/days; Afghanistan/Pakistan;
hospital/school; $120,000/$12,000; oldest/
wisest; four/three; $5 million/$1 million

UNDERSTANDING WORD GROUPS

write, five, meters

FINDING MORE INFORMATION

2. d
3. e
4. g
5. c
6. a
7. b

UNIT 6

THE SONG

Page 52: The words *dream, dreams,* and *dreamed*
appear in the song ten times.

Page 53: The third verse has no words that rhyme.

Story 11: Susan's Got Talent

VOCABULARY

1. clapping
2. shock
3. although
4. bullied

UNDERSTANDING THE MAIN IDEAS

2. April 11, 2009
3. famous
4. middle-aged, gray
5. 47
6. professional singer
7. incredible
8. 100 million times

UNDERSTANDING WORD GROUPS

fist, surprised, reply, help, wow

REMEMBERING DETAILS

When she was born, she didn't get enough oxygen.

It was difficult for her to learn.

The children at school teased and bullied her.

Whenever she felt sad or lonely, she sang.

She tried to become a professional singer several
times.

She took care of her mother for years.

Story 12: The King in the Nursing Home

VOCABULARY

2. old
3. 80
4. with other people
5. money
6. school

UNDERSTANDING THE MAIN IDEAS

2. a
3. b
4. c
5. c
6. a

UNDERSTANDING TIME RELATIONSHIPS

2. e
3. a
4. d
5. c

UNDERSTANDING CONTRASTS

U.S.: a small apartment, patients, supervisors, a
nursing home, coworkers

RWENZURURU: a green robe, security guards, a
large house, a suit

UNIT 7

THE SONG

The line *follow the drinking gourd* is in the song 23
times.

Story 13: The Drinking Gourd

VOCABULARY

2. f
3. a
4. d
5. b
6. g
7. e

UNDERSTANDING THE MAIN IDEAS

1. b
2. c

REMEMBERING DETAILS

A. They lived in the South.
   They lived on plantations.
   They worked in cotton and sugar fields.
B. He was old.
   He did small jobs on the plantations.
   Part of one leg was missing.
   In the evenings, he sang with the slaves.

CHECKING FACTS

TRUE: 1, 2, 4, 5
NOT SURE: 3, 6

Story 14: Twelve Kilometers to a New Life

VOCABULARY

1. OK
2. clothes
3. △
4. grass
5. cooking and heating
6. 2 A.M.
7. 12

REVIEWING THE STORY

2. West
3. balloon
4. fabric
5. cloud
6. meters
7. took
8. side

REMEMBERING DETAILS

cut the fabric into big triangles.
sew the pieces together to make a balloon.
make a passenger basket out of wood.
take the balloon to a meadow.
heat the air in the balloon with propane gas.
fly over the wall.

FINDING MORE INFORMATION

2. e
3. d
4. f
5. a
6. c

UNIT 8

Story 15: The Littlest Passenger

VOCABULARY

2. crew
3. hesitated
4. rescued
5. nursing home

REMEMBERING DETAILS

It carried more than 2,000 passengers.
It had a swimming pool, a gym, and a library.
It hit an iceberg on the fourth night of its first voyage.
It sank three hours after it hit the iceberg.
It didn't have enough lifeboats for all its passengers.

UNDERSTANDING CAUSE AND EFFECT

2. b
3. d
4. a
5. f
6. e

UNDERSTANDING TIME SEQUENCE

2. The *Titanic* hit an iceberg.
3. The *Titanic* sank.
4. The survivors of the *Titanic* arrived in New York City.
5. The last survivor of the *Titanic* died.

Story 16: Miracle on the Hudson

VOCABULARY

2. unhappy
3. want
4. air
5. can't
6. good

UNDERSTANDING DETAILS

1522/1549; Los Angeles/New York; minutes/
seconds; ducks/geese; copilot/pilot; 14/42;
Mexico/Jersey; Mississippi/Hudson; 15/150;
first/last; Helicopters/Boats

UNDERSTANDING DIALOG

engines   runway
land   like
right, Airport   Hudson

UNDERSTANDING WORD GROUPS

chairs, angry, cows, holiday, ship

ACKNOWLEDGMENTS

I WISH TO THANK:

- my students at the Whitewater (WI) Community Education Adult ESL Program, who gave me their honest opinions of the songs, stories, and exercises. I would like to thank Carmen Valverde Diaz, José Luis Gaytán, and Antonia V. Villalva in particular for providing the writing examples;

- Jessie Dugan and Katherine Conover, my colleagues at the Whitewater (WI) Community Education Adult ESL Program, who generously opened their classrooms to me so that I could fieldtest material while they observed. Their suggestions for improving the stories and exercises have been invaluable;

- Sue Sesolak, Joyce Besserer, and Jennifer Esh at Waukesha (WI) County Technical College, who also generously shared their wonderful students with me so that I could fieldtest materials at their site;

- Sharron Bassano, my former colleague at the Santa Cruz Adult School, who developed the type of discussion/writing activity found in many units. I have used her draw/write/speak sequence to structure class discussions many times, always with great success, and am indebted to her for sharing it;

- Pietro Alongi at Pearson Education, who responded to my proposal for this book by enthusiastically sketching layout ideas on a paper napkin. His subsequent suggestions helped shape the book's form and focus;

- Debbie Sistino at Pearson Education, who generously shared her editorial expertise and walked through the permissions labyrinth with me;

- Karen Davy, whose editorial skill and experience were, as always, greatly appreciated;

- Christopher Leonowicz at Pearson Education, who guided this book through its final stages with great care;

- Minnesota Literacy Council's Tutor Resource Center, the source of the discussion/writing activity that follows Story 2 ("Draw My Room");

- Laurel Pollard and Natalie Hess, authors of *Zero Prep* (Alta Book Center Publishers, 1997). The teaching tip for Story 1 is based on an activity in that book ("Poems for Students by Students," page 93), as is the discussion/writing exercise following Story 7 ("Rules to Live By," page 12);

- Chris Gunn, who contributed the idea for Story 15's discussion/writing exercise on the website Lanternfish ("Movie Riddles: An ESL Activity to Get Students Talking about Movies");

- Kristin Lems, who demonstrated several of the listening activities at TESOL 2009 (in a presentation titled "Using Music to Teach ESL");

- Kathy Olson, who demonstrated several of the post-reading activities suggested in the To the Teacher section at TESOL 2007 (in a presentation titled "Repetition: Multiple Activities Using One Reading Selection");

- John Hajdu Heyer—musician, musicologist, and husband extraordinaire—who was the first reader of every story and the first listener to every song.

Song Credits